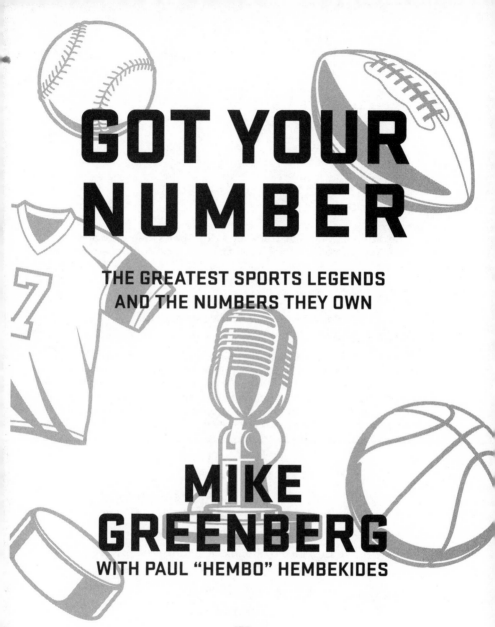

GOT YOUR NUMBER

THE GREATEST SPORTS LEGENDS AND THE NUMBERS THEY OWN

MIKE GREENBERG

WITH PAUL "HEMBO" HEMBEKIDES

HYPERION AVENUE

LOS ANGELES   NEW YORK

The authors would like to acknowledge Sports Reference and ESPN Stats & Information as invaluable resources for the research that went into this book.

First Edition, April 2023

10 9 8 7 6 5 4 3 2 1

FAC-004510-23048

Printed in the United States of America

This book is set in Museo Slab

Designed by Stephanie Sumulong

Cataloging-in-Publication Control Number 2022940155

ISBN 978-1-368-07356-1

Reinforced binding

www.HyperionAvenueBooks.com

SUSTAINABLE FORESTRY INITIATIVE
Certified Sourcing
www.sfiprogram.org
SFI-01681

Logo Applies to Text Stock Only

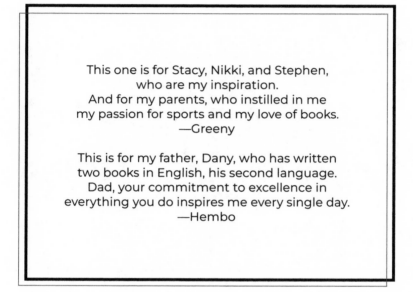

This one is for Stacy, Nikki, and Stephen,
who are my inspiration.
And for my parents, who instilled in me
my passion for sports and my love of books.
—Greeny

This is for my father, Dany, who has written
two books in English, his second language.
Dad, your commitment to excellence in
everything you do inspires me every single day.
—Hembo

INTRODUCTION

SO, I SUPPOSE YOU'RE WONDERING WHY I'VE ASKED YOU HERE.

The year was 1985, and I was a freshman at Northwestern University in Evanston, Illinois. The lecture hall was vast and dimly lit, the smell of coffee and nervous anticipation in the air. It was the first day of classes—my first day as a college student. The class was called Introduction to Philosophy. I was seated in the back, having carefully selected a spot behind a very tall man so as not to run any risk of being called upon. The professor entered from a side door I hadn't previously noticed and took his place beneath a giant screen. The room went silent as he shuffled papers at the lectern. After an extended moment, he tapped his microphone a time or two and then blew into it loudly.

"My fellow scholars," he said. "I want you to consider the following idea: that the only questions that are really worth asking in life are those to which we will never know the answer."

The following day, I dropped his class.

His idea was so foreign to my way of thinking, such complete anathema to my view of what makes life fun, that I simply could not allow myself to be subjected to whatever his next idea might be. All these years later, I still haven't gotten over the first one.

You see, I am a sports talk-show host. In my job, there is no question that cannot be answered. In most cases those answers come loudly, immediately, and with considerable bombast. In fact, if there was a handbook for sports talk-show hosts, the first rule would be: No matter the question, always have an answer. The second rule would be: Your opinion is always right. And the third: In the event you are wrong, see rule number two.

I have been doing this job for more than thirty years, and in that time those rules have very much built nests in my sensibility. Taking a position on a topic in sports and being fully prepared to defend it is not just something I am accustomed to; it is my way of life. It is practically my reason for being.

In the three decades I have been building up that muscle memory, opining loudly on radio and television, the questions I am asked most frequently on golf courses, city streets, and in airports always begin: *Hey, Greeny, who do you think is better . . .*

Not a day goes by that I don't hear those words. The waiter in the restaurant, the Uber driver, the guy behind me in line at Starbucks, they all want to know who I think is better. And, invariably, whomever I choose, they think I am wrong.

At their essence, sports lend themselves to the most good-natured debate you will ever encounter, because there is nothing in the world better than investing everything in something that means absolutely nothing. When someone asks me whether I think LeBron James is better than Michael Jordan, the consequences of my response mean nothing—there are literally zero stakes—and yet both of us know that my answer also means absolutely everything.

That is the nature of sports conversation: heated debate with zero consequence.

I would know; I've been doing it all my life.

And I love it.

Honestly, I wish more of the discourse in our society could be this way. Lord knows, our political discourse is hardly ever a fraction as polite, or productive, as the sessions being conducted every day on sports radio stations across states both red and blue. When I was a boy, I was taught that sports brought people together like nothing else, the old adage about the millionaire and the taxi driver on adjacent barstools watching the ball game as equals. It hasn't always been that way lately, of course, but I continue to believe sports debate remains about the most reasonable and respectful watercooler talk that we have in American society.

So, this book is about that, first and foremost—about the creation of a hundred sports debates that we can engage in respectfully. Which is to say, I will offer my opinions and you will likely agree with some of them and disagree with others. You will sometimes be convinced I am wrong. At those times, I ask you to please remember that mine is that rare genius that will not be fully appreciated until well after I'm out of the picture.

I can't think of a better way to spend our time.

But this book is about something more than that as well, something much bigger. Because sports have always been about more than that, at least for me. These games that people play have always felt disproportionately meaningful in my life.

Nothing makes me feel more comfortable, or more at home, than talking about sports.

You probably feel that way, too. If you were moved to buy this book, or someone was moved to buy it for you, it had to be with the knowledge that all this stuff means as much to you as it does to me. In that way, sports conversation is something far greater and more meaningful than how it is typically portrayed. It is something that taps into the deepest parts of our souls. It is about our connection to all that has come before, and all those who were with us to experience it. Sports are about our childhood, our family, our youth.

Simply put: Sports are about memories, which by definition took place in the past, which explains why for sports fans the past was always the best time. This is a universal rule that applies to every sports fan, always has and, I believe, always will.

I can prove it to you. Tell me how old you are, and I will tell you how you will respond to almost any sports question. Seven times out of ten I will be right. (And you will be wrong on the other three.)

For example, my father would always drop Oscar Robertson into any discussion about how good Michael Jordan was, in exactly the same way I now drop Michael into any conversation about how good LeBron James is. I guarantee you that thirty years from now, my son will do the same for LeBron, when his son or daughter talks about how good whoever becomes the next Greatest Of All Time (G.O.A.T.) is. Invariably, those discussions will ascend into arguments.

(Note: *ascend*, as opposed to *descend*. Sports is the only milieu in which debate is the highest form of conversation. It pains me to say it, all these years later, but maybe that philosophy professor was onto something. Maybe the truth is that the questions really worth asking, at least in sports, are the ones that engender a lifetime worth of debate.)

Hopefully, this book will prove fodder in elevating those debates, along with the ones your sons and daughters will have with their children. I can think of no greater legacy a sports fan can have than passing down our passions to the next generation of season-ticket holders, face-painters, and stubborn debaters.

Bless their hearts, they have their priorities in order.

SO, WHAT DOES THIS HAVE TO DO WITH NUMBERS ANYWAY?

It was during the height of Covid, and I was in Bristol, Connecticut, where we moved the headquarters of *Get Up* when they shut down our studios in New York. Most days after the show, the few members of the staff who were still working in the office sat around and talked about sports, in part because we are a bunch of sports geeks, but also because there just wasn't anywhere to hurry off to at that time. One day, I recall, we tried to name the placekicker on every NFL team in 1977, and I am somewhat ashamed to admit that we accomplished it. (Rich Szaro and Horst Muhlmann did their best to trip us up, but in the end we would not be denied.)

Anyway, one morning we tried to identify the uniform number of every quarterback in the Pro Football Hall of Fame. Again, we succeeded; in fact this one we found quite easy, largely because so many of the quarterbacks wore the same number. For example, the following all wore jersey number 12: Terry Bradshaw, Bob Griese, Jim Kelly, Joe Namath, Ken Stabler, Roger Staubach.

The executive producer of *Get Up* is named Pete McConville. He and I are (by far) the oldest members of the staff, and thus the ones to whom this game was most appealing. And it was Pete who asked aloud the question that ultimately became the central thesis of this book.

"They all *wore* number 12," he said, "but which one *owns* the number 12?"

Instantly, two things happened. First, everyone in the room agreed Tom Brady owns that number. Second, I realized that this question was the perfect subject for a book.

So, that is where this idea comes from and that is what it is: the very simple, vague, nebulous, indistinct, purely subjective concept of which person in sports deserves ownership of every number, 1 through 100. With painstaking research from my right-hand man, Paul Hembekides (the legendary "Hembo"), and apologies to absolutely no one, here come the honorable hundred (and then some) owners of the most prestigious touchstones in the entire world of sports.

SO, WHERE DID THESE NUMBERS COME FROM, ANYWAY?

According to a report in the *Brisbane Courier*, on the afternoon of July 17, 1897, sports as we know them were forever changed by a rugby match between Queensland and New Zealand, with players having numbers on their uniforms for the first time in recorded history. Numbers were first mandated as part of the uniform fourteen years later, also in Australia, this time in New South Wales, in the sport of "Association Football," or Australian rules football as we know it today.

It was another five years later when, in 1916, the Cleveland

Indians became the first team in Major League Baseball to attach numbers to the jerseys of their players; they put them on the players' left sleeves. The players didn't like it, and just as quickly the numbers were taken off. The legendary Tris Speaker hit .386 for the Indians that year; in no photo from that season or any other is he seen with a number anywhere on his uniform.

In 1929, the Indians gave jersey numbers another go, a few days later the Yankees did the same, and within ten years every Major League Baseball team followed suit. The Yankees handed out numbers based upon a player's spot in the batting order, which is how Babe Ruth acquired the number 3. His teammate, Lou Gehrig, hit cleanup, and his number, 4, became the first ever retired by any team on July 4, 1939, the day he called himself "the luckiest man on the face of the earth."

In the nine decades that have passed since, uniform numbers have become an essential part of sports currency. Many fans will as frequently remember a player's uniform number as their first name. Coaches regularly refer to players by their number, as do teammates, opponents, and commentators. And, worn correctly, the numbers themselves often become an essential piece of a player's identity.

Players today wear uniform numbers in practically every team sport across the globe, from cricket to handball to field hockey. Race car drivers are indelibly linked to the numbers on their cars, although in NASCAR the numbers are the property of the owner of the racing team, not the individual driver. In water polo, numerals are on the swim caps. In horse racing, a wager is usually placed on "the eight horse in the third race."

So, numbers are an incredibly vital piece in the grand jigsaw puzzle of sports. Increasingly so, as a matter of fact. Analytics (advanced statistical analysis) has actually opened doors for countless new devotees to find careers in the industry, men and women drawn to the mathematical probabilities that guide decision-making, most of whom are built a lot more like Mike Greenberg than Mike Tyson. (Brief aside: In my childhood, there were no Daryl Moreys; had I known there was a path like that for me, I would have chosen it.) Analytics has made sports more interesting to a gigantic swath of the population that may never have paid attention before, finding a fascination for numbers they might not have had for the athleticism or the drama. Legalized gambling is still another avenue that has popularized the numbers attached to sports, inspiring students, soccer moms, and social studies teachers alike to learn about point spreads and tournament brackets. At this point, numbers could no more be exorcised from sports than could personal trainers or hyperbaric chambers.

However, of all the ways numbers and sports have become inextricably linked, I would argue that uniform numbers are the most lasting and profound.

If you are inclined to argue, "No, Greeny, statistics are more intrinsic than uniform numbers!" allow this to be the first of many times we are going to disagree amid these pages.

I make my case with the following list of questions:

How many points did Michael Jordan score?
How many hits did Pete Rose have?
How many home runs did Barry Bonds hit?
How many touchdowns did Joe Montana throw?
How many goals did Wayne Gretzky score?
And, finally, what uniform numbers did they all wear?

Raise your hand if the only question on this list you could answer is the last one. Come on, be honest.

The point of this exercise is not to make you or me feel or sound dumb, but rather to point out how obscure and, at times, inconsequential statistics feel.

And thus, if we now agree that uniform numbers are the most essential digits in all of sports, we can safely proceed to our next order of business.

SO, HOW ARE WE CHOOSING THE WINNERS HERE?

Let's make one thing perfectly clear: *We* are not choosing anything here. I am.

I alone am choosing, based on the criteria I deem most important. There is both an art and a science to assigning greatness in sports, and I plan to use both, in equal measure.

There are, in fact, many and varied ways in which we can define greatness in sports, and I plan to take them all into consideration. Those attributes include, but are not limited to: accomplishment, physical talent, mental toughness, game intelligence, courage, clutchness, impact on the sport, impact on society, iconic moments, sportsmanship, citizenship, and joy.

That last one is big for me. I want to see my favorite athletes joyous when they compete. I want to feel that they appreciate how blessed they are to be where they are, doing what they are doing. Somewhere inside they recognize and acknowledge how the rest of us would beg, borrow, or steal to trade places with them, if only for a day. Don't get me wrong, that disposition is not a prerequisite to being great in a sport, but it is an absolute must to claim a coveted spot in this book.

"Go crazy, folks! Go crazy!"

With those words, the iconic broadcaster Jack Buck painted the perfect finishing touch onto perhaps the most improbable home run in the history of baseball.

The date was October 14, 1985, game five of the National League Championship Series between the Cardinals and the Dodgers, tied at two in the bottom of the ninth in St. Louis. The Dodgers' pitcher was Tom Niedenfuer, in relief of Fernando Valenzuela. The count was one ball, two strikes. The home run was hit left-handed by the Cardinals' shortstop, Ozzie Smith, wearing number 1. To that point in his career, Smith had taken 3,009 at-bats lefty and never hit a single home run. But he hit one that late Monday afternoon to win the biggest game of the year. That's the best thing about baseball—sometimes the impossible happens.

Ozzie Smith played a position that doesn't exist in the sport anymore. He played shortstop at a time when that was the most important position on the field, and all that mattered was how well you played it defensively—and Smith played it better than anyone else ever. In fact, Ozzie Smith, known as the Wizard of Oz, played shortstop as well as anyone in the history of the game ever did *anything*. He won the Gold Glove in thirteen consecutive seasons; Omar Vizquel has the next most at the game's most demanding position with nine. Consider: The most consecutive seasons in which Babe Ruth led the American League in home runs was six. The most consecutive seasons in which either Randy Johnson or Nolan Ryan led either league

> # OZZIE SMITH played shortstop as well as anyone in the history of the game ever did *anything*.

in strikeouts was four. Being the best at anything every season for a decade-plus is extraordinarily rare in any sport, much less baseball, much less the most demanding position on the diamond. Further, all those seasons Smith played shortstop at Busch Stadium were on the synthetic concrete known as Astroturf, subjecting him to a level of wear and tear that (blessedly) no player will ever endure again.

Having said all of that, I would next point out that those details are just numbers, and that to watch Ozzie Smith play shortstop was to know that numbers could never fully capture the experience. Smith was an artist, as graceful as any dancer, as flexible as any gymnast. There was something genuinely beautiful about watching him play the position he redefined in the '80s, a position that would never be the same again once his career was done. That's because Cal Ripken Jr., who next assumed the mantle of baseball's best shortstop from Smith, redefined it again, beginning the transition toward raw power, which has characterized the position since. Consider: Ripken hit as many home runs in his first full season in the big leagues, 28, as Smith hit in his entire career. Alex Rodriguez hit more home runs than that in seven of his eight full seasons as a shortstop, including more than twice as many, 57, in 2002. The point being, not only was there never anyone quite like Ozzie Smith, there will never be anyone like him again. It's like he perfected the position to the point that the position itself had to change going forward.

Ozzie Smith represents something that made the game great that we have lost forever and miss terribly. What a shame that is for the game of baseball and all of us who love it. His legacy will live forever here, though. There is only one Ozzie Smith, and the number 1 belongs to him.

Merriam-Webster dictionaries define *clutch,* when used as an adjective, as "successful in a crucial situation." My unsolicited advice to them is to use an image to reinforce that definition—a photo of Derek Jeter playing baseball.

How does one acquire that mysterious quality—one that only the most select few in sports possess—of being at one's very best in the most important moments? How does one quantify the value of that quality to a team, or a fan base, or a sport itself? The answer is actually more simple than you might think: Being clutch is absolutely everything.

And, unfortunately for many, clutchness itself is something you are either born with or you are not. There is no teaching it, there is no learning it.

Derek Jeter was not the greatest baseball player of his generation; he wasn't even particularly close. But the moments he created, the leadership he displayed, the championships he

YOUR ATTENTION, PLEASE, LADIES AND GENTLEMEN;
NOW BATTING FOR THE YANKEES, NUMBER 2,

DEREK JETER.

willed his team toward, and his almost superhuman charisma combined to make him something more like a phenomenon than an athlete, a true living legend. As of this writing, Jeter remains the most popular player in his sport according to the ESPN Fan and Media Intelligence group—some six years after he played his final game.

The home run Jeter hit after midnight in a game that began on Halloween night earned him the nickname Mr. November, but the truth is no player ever accomplished more in October. Jeter is baseball's all-time postseason leader in games, hits, runs, and total bases. He is the only player ever to hit .350 or better in four World Series. His teams went 97–61 in playoff games, a win percentage of better than 61 percent over the equivalent of a full season in the most important games against only the best teams. His Yankees had plenty of stars, but they had only one leader, one captain. Derek Jeter was the face of all those teams and the face of our national pastime for a generation. The respect he earned from teammates, opponents, fans—even from Yankee haters—has been unequaled in the sport.

The legendary public address announcer Bob Sheppard used to welcome the shortstop to the plate at Yankee Stadium with the simplest of words: *Your attention, please, ladies and gentlemen; now batting for the Yankees, number 2, Derek Jeter.*

Number 2. That simple phrase became so iconic that every baseball fan can still hear it in any quiet moment. His uniform number was such an intrinsic part of his identity that it will serve as Jeter's introduction for as long as the game is played. It is only fitting that the number 2 should belong to Derek Jeter, now and forever.

In 1930, Herbert Hoover, the president of the United States, earned a salary of seventy thousand dollars. That same year, Babe Ruth, wearing number 3 for the New York Yankees, signed a contract that paid him eighty thousand. When asked if he thought it appropriate that a ballplayer should make more money than the leader of the free world, Ruth said, "Why not? I had a better year than he did."

It's not bragging if it is the truth. While he himself probably wouldn't have used the word, Babe Ruth was the originator of swag.

George Herman Ruth was much more than the greatest slugger in the history of the major leagues—which he indisputably was. Consider that in 1920 Ruth hit 54 home runs, more than any other team in the American League. Further, from 1926 to 1932 Ruth hit 343 home runs, while five different teams hit fewer in total. It's ridiculous. Meanwhile, Ruth was, of course, also an extraordinary pitcher. He led the league with a 1.75 ERA in 1916 and won all three of his career World Series starts, allowing only 3 runs in 31 innings. And, most important of all, Ruth was a winner: The Yankees, who had never won a title before his arrival, captured seven pennants and four World Series during his fifteen seasons in New York.

But all those statistics, gargantuan though they may be, do not begin to tell the story of the significance of the man behind them. Ruth elevated the role a sportsman could play in our society. He rescued a sport reeling from the 1919 World Series gambling scandal. He singlehandedly popularized the

> **BABE RUTH** was the originator of swag.

practice of autographing baseballs, once joking that balls *not* signed by him were a rarity. He was a prolific pitchman: Ruth endorsed underwear, candy, sporting goods, Wheaties, shaving cream, razor blades, and chewing tobacco. He toured in a vaudeville act. The ballpark in which he played most of his career, venerable Yankee Stadium, was commonly known as the House that Ruth Built. Ruth's fame also extended well beyond American shores: During World War II the *New York Times* reported that Japanese troops charging US soldiers were yelling, "To hell with Babe Ruth!"

At the turn of the last century, *Life* magazine listed the most influential Americans of the twentieth century. Four athletes made the list: Ruth, Muhammad Ali, Billie Jean King, and

Jackie Robinson. Worthy of note is that Ruth's career ended before Ali or King were even born—but nobody came along that could knock him off that list. Babe Ruth blazed a trail superstar athletes traverse in this country to this very day. He is as important to the culture of the United States as just about any athlete who ever lived. As the Bambino himself (as played by Art LaFleur) says in the much-beloved movie *The Sandlot:* "Heroes get remembered, but legends never die."

The date was May 10, 1970, the location was the iconic Boston Garden, and the anticipation was feverish. The Bruins were on the verge of sweeping the Blues in the Stanley Cup Final. Boston had dominated the series, winning the first three games by a combined twelve goals, but game four was much more competitive, ultimately requiring overtime. Forty seconds into that extra session, the best player in the world, Boston defenseman Bobby Orr, flashed in front of the net. As he shot the puck past future Hall of Fame goalie Glenn Hall, he was upended by Noel Picard; Orr appeared to be flying through the air as the fans began celebrating the team's first championship in twenty-nine years. The photo of Orr soaring horizontally past the net remains far and away the most iconic image in the history of hockey. Forty years later to the day, the Bruins would unveil a bronze statue of that moment outside their arena, assuring its immortality.

Of course, Bobby Orr was a lot more than just one unforgettable moment. He was without question the greatest defenseman of all time, and a reasonable argument could be made that he was the second-best hockey player ever to live, behind only Wayne Gretzky. Consider: Orr is the only player in history to win all four major awards of his sport (the Art Ross, Hart, Norris, and Conn Smythe trophies); he won each of them at least twice, and, remarkably, once won *all* of them in a single season (1969–70). He is the only defenseman to lead the league in points scored, which he did twice as well. He was the first player, at any position, to win three consecutive MVPs. He

> **BOBBY ORR** was without question the best defenseman of all time.

had six seasons in which he tallied at least 100 points; all other defensemen in history have combined for eight such seasons. His plus/minus was plus-80 in four different seasons; Wayne Gretzky achieved that only twice, and no other player ever did it more than once. Orr's mark of plus-124 in the 1970–71 season is a record that stands to this day.

Perhaps most remarkable of all Orr's achievements is how he managed to accomplish so much in so little time. His style of play was hard on his knees, which gave out on him at a young age; Orr played only 36 games after the season in which he turned 26, and he retired at 30. Still, the mark he left on the sport was indestructible. The mandatory waiting period for the Hall of Fame was waived for him, and in 1979 he was enshrined at the age of 31, the youngest player ever inducted. It was around that time that the *Boston Globe* ran a poll of New Englanders asking to name the greatest player in Boston sports history; Orr finished first, ahead of Ted Williams, Bill Russell, Carl Yastrzemski, and Bob Cousy. On the night his jersey number, 4, was lifted to the rafters at Boston Garden, the fans gave him a standing ovation that lasted eleven minutes.

Simply put, the game of hockey can be divided into two eras: the time before Bobby Orr played, and the time since. Perhaps no one ever summed that up better than Frank Deford when he wrote in *Sports Illustrated*, "It's not necessary to get into who may be better, Orr, the defenseman, or Wayne Gretzky, the center, except to note that Orr did something that Gretzky had no opportunity to do, and that was change the very nature of the game."

It was April 1951, and Joseph Paul DiMaggio was beginning what would be his final season as a New York Yankee. He had played twelve years already, and it was noticeable (and noteworthy) to everyone just how hard he continued to play every time he stepped onto a field. A reporter asked him about it, wondering why the legendary outfielder never seemed to give anything less than every ounce he had. "Because," DiMaggio said, "there is always some kid who may be seeing me for the first time. I owe him my best."

In the entire recorded history of quotations emanating from the world of sports, that one is my favorite.

Where to begin describing the genius of Joe DiMaggio? He played thirteen seasons and was an all-star in every one of them. He won nine World Series and reached another. His teams averaged 98 wins, when a season was only 154 games long. DiMaggio hit 361 home runs and would likely have hit a hundred more had he not missed *three full seasons* at his absolute peak (ages twenty-eight to thirty) serving our nation during World War II. Unimaginably, DiMaggio struck out only 369 times during his career, and never 40 times in any one season. The 56-game hitting streak he achieved in 1941 remains arguably the game's most sacred and cherished record.

During baseball's centennial in 1969, DiMaggio was voted the greatest living ballplayer, and was introduced as such the rest of his life. His legend was perhaps second only to Ruth's in the history of the sport; so many references to him in popular culture remain iconic to this day. Les Brown named him "Joltin' Joe DiMaggio" in song. Paul Simon poignantly asked, "Where have you gone, Joe DiMaggio? A nation turns its lonely eyes to you." DiMaggio was half of sport's first power couple, married to Marilyn Monroe at the absolute peak of her stardom. Ernest Hemingway wrote of him with wonder and awe

Where to begin describing the genius of **JOE DiMAGGIO**?

in his classic *The Old Man and the Sea*. Very few sportsmen have inspired anywhere near the reverence Joe DiMaggio did during his career.

For me, there is also a more personal connection. My father, from whom I inherited much of my passion for sports, was raised in the Bronx at the exact height of DiMaggio's career. His admiration was such that when my dad's first book was published, he dedicated it to the heroes who were his inspiration, naming DiMaggio alongside Clarence Darrow and William O. Douglas. Any time I have been privileged to throw out a pitch at a stadium, or participate in any other baseball activities, I have always worn the number 5 as a tribute to both my dad and his idol. And when my kids began to play sports, any time they were allowed to select a uniform, they always chose 5 as well.

There were a lot of difficult choices to be made in this book regarding who has won which number, but for me this was the easiest of them all. Joe DiMaggio owns the number 5, and he always will.

Vince Lombardi famously said: "Winning isn't everything, it's the only thing." I have never fully understood what to make of that quote. Perhaps I should have asked Bill Russell, because if anyone would ever have known, it would have been him.

Russell was, inarguably, the greatest winner in the history of American team sports. That story begins in 1955, when he joined the University of San Francisco and earned them back-to-back NCAA championships. Russell was named the Most Outstanding Player of the 1955 Final Four, and became the first collegian ever to average 20 points and 20 rebounds for his career. USF went 57–1 over those two seasons, becoming the first ever unbeaten national champs in 1956. Russell also captained the United States team at the Olympics that year and would later call his gold medal "probably my most prized possession." From there, Russell would join the Boston

Celtics and lead that team to eleven NBA championships in his thirteen seasons as a player—those eleven titles remain the most by any player ever. So, let me do the math for you: Over a fifteen-season span from 1955 to 1969, William Felton Russell won two NCAA championships, eleven NBA titles, and an Olympic gold medal—all while wearing the number 6. It is probably safe to assume that is a stretch of winning that has never been equaled and likely never will be again.

Amazingly, the numbers do not end there. Consider this: Bill Russell played twenty-one winner-take-all games in his career (including all NBA best-of-five and best-of-seven, all NCAA tournament games, and all Olympic medal rounds)—and he

> # BILL RUSSELL was the greatest winner in the history of American team sports.

won *every one of them.* Ten of those were NBA game sevens, and in those he played 488 of a possible 495 minutes and averaged 29.3 rebounds. Russell was named the league's MVP five times, a mark matched by Michael Jordan and surpassed only by Kareem Abdul-Jabbar's six. His rebounding numbers are the stuff of legend, but worthy of note is that blocked shots did not become an official statistic until after his career ended. The NBA record for games with at least 10 blocks is nineteen, held by Mark Eaton. It has been estimated that Russell had two hundred games with 10 blocked shots—if properly recorded, that would be one of those records in sports guaranteed to never be broken.

Perhaps all you really need to know about Russell's reputation for winning is that the NBA Finals MVP is named in his honor.

Still, if that is all you know of Bill Russell, then you don't know the most important part of his story. In 1961, Russell and several of his Black teammates were denied service at their hotel in Lexington, Kentucky. They decided not to play the game. Bill Russell's impact in the area of racial equality and social justice is the most indelible element of his legacy. Far more has been written on his magnitude than could ever be done justice here; suffice it to say, he was so admired that in 2011 he received the Presidential Medal of Freedom, the foremost US civilian decoration, awarded to individuals who have made "an especially meritorious contribution to the national interests of the United States."

Bill Russell is deserving of a place on the all-time Mount Rushmore of basketball, and he is undoubtedly the owner of the number 6. And, delightfully, the NBA agrees. Shortly after I concluded writing this essay, Commissioner Adam Silver announced the unprecedented step of retiring the number in Russell's honor league wide. There is no greater tribute a sports league can pay to a legend, nor any legend more deserving of the recognition.

From their founding in the AFL in 1960 through the 1982 season, no football team lost more games than the Denver Broncos. And then, John Elway happened. The quarterback that analyst Mel Kiper Jr. described as the greatest quarterback prospect in history traveled a mile high and achieved the impossible by exceeding everyone's lofty expectations. Almost immediately, Elway reversed the narrative for the hapless Broncos; no quarterback won more games in the 1980s and 1990s than he did. A franchise with just two playoff wins in the first twenty-three years of their existence became a powerhouse, and the strong-armed signal caller with the huge smile became their first superstar.

Putting it plainly, John Elway *was* the Broncos: Consider that during his sixteen seasons he was responsible for 334 touchdowns (300 passing, 33 rushing, 1 receiving) and thus generated 4,771 of the team's 5,806 points scored—more than

82 percent of the total. He led the previously perennial losers to fourteen playoff wins, including five AFC championship victories. As of this writing, only Tom Brady has started more Super Bowls at quarterback than Elway.

The first three Super Bowls to which Elway led the Broncos were unprecedentedly disastrous; they lost the games by a combined 96 points. (Incidentally, the first lede I ever wrote professionally was on the night of their 55–10 loss in Super Bowl XXIV. "The Denver Broncos won the opening coin toss and should have elected to go home." I remain proud of that one.)

> # It is hard to imagine there will ever be an athlete as beloved in any city as **JOHN ELWAY** is in Denver.

At the time, and to this day, it remains my contention that anyone who holds those defeats against Elway's historical ledger couldn't be more off base. The accomplishment of dragging what were, candidly, mediocre supporting casts like lambs into a series of slaughters was, in fact, a testament to his greatness. There were far better teams in the AFC in each of those seasons; they just didn't have John Elway.

It was not until Elway's fifteenth season that his team finally scaled the mountain—that wait remains (as of this writing) the longest by any former MVP with his original team in any of the four major sports. Super Bowl XXXII, Denver's upset of heavily favored Green Bay, is memorable for any number of reasons, highlighted by Elway's famed "helicopter dive." But it was the four-word phrase spoken by Pat Bowlen at the end that will be remembered forever. Standing on the victors' podium, surrounded by jubilant players and coaches, the owner of the franchise raised high the Lombardi Trophy and shouted "This one's for John!"

Indeed it was.

A year later, in his final game, Elway won it again, a second Super Bowl for a franchise that had just two playoff wins before his arrival. At 38 years and 217 days old, he was the oldest quarterback ever to win the title (a mark surpassed by Peyton Manning, after Elway recruited him to Denver). Elway threw for 336 yards in that final game and was named the MVP—the first Hall of Fame quarterback to finish his career with a Super Bowl win. It was a fitting finish for a man who carried the burden of expectation and the weight of an entire franchise on his shoulders for nearly two decades. It is hard to imagine there will ever be an athlete as beloved in any city as John Elway is in Denver; he may be as synonymous with that city as any athlete has ever been anywhere. And he is richly deserving of that honor—in a crowded field, the lucky number 7 belongs to him.

Describing his mindset during competition, Kobe Bryant once said, "My brain cannot process failure." That is, of course, the perfect description of the Mamba Mentality; no player in NBA history ever missed more shots, and no player was ever more certain the *next one* was going in.

The truth is one could argue for Kobe owning two places in this book. He played exactly half his career wearing the number 8, then switched to 24, ten seasons in each, and his stats were startlingly identical in both decades of play, a testament to his remarkable consistency and dedication. I chose 8 for him because he won three of his five titles in that jersey—even if the two he won later, without Shaquille O'Neal, might ultimately mean more for his NBA legacy.

We don't have the space to present a comprehensive list of Kobe's accomplishments, so here are just a select few:

- five-time NBA champion

THERE HAVE BEEN PRECIOUS FEW ATHLETES WHO
HAVE BEEN REVERED BY THEIR PEERS IN THE WAY

KOBE BRYANT

WAS, AND IS, AND LIKELY WILL BE FOREVER.

- two-time Finals MVP
- two-time Olympic gold medalist
- eighteen-time NBA All-Star
- fifteen-time All-NBA selection
- twelve-time All-Defensive selection

Kobe gave us so many nights that we will never forget. The night he dropped 61 at Madison Square Garden. The night he scored 81 against Toronto. The iconic alley-oop he threw to Shaq to beat Portland en route to his first championship. The game seven when he finally beat Boston. The sixty he scored in his final game—but mostly the way he took the microphone afterward and offered the perfect punctuation for the final night of his career, closing with the words "Mamba Out."

There have been precious few athletes who have been revered by their peers in the way Kobe was, and is, and likely will be forever. His determination, unwavering self-belief, and extraordinary charisma combined to make him one of the most respected players to ever wear *any* uniform.

The last time I saw Kobe was in March 2019. He was in New York promoting his book series for young adults. We met in a private area of the NBA Store on Fifth Avenue for an interview that lasted about a half hour. What was most striking in the conversation was how little he wanted to talk about his career, his place in history, his past life. He had very much moved on and was notably more excited talking about all the opportunities that lay ahead. He was a young man with a lot of living left to do.

Like you, I will never forget where I was on January 26, 2020. I spent the morning playing golf in Tampa, a weekend getaway from the cold weather in New York. I was in a car headed to the airport when the texts started to come, first as a trickle, then a storm. The tragic death of Kobe Bryant at the age of forty-one shook the world of sports in ways I have seldom seen in my three decades in the industry. It seemed impossible he was really gone. Sometimes it still does. There will come a time, I am sure, when we will take great joy in watching highlights of his play. For me, that time has not yet come. Suffice it then to say simply that Kobe is an easy choice for this book, as one of the greatest athletes and legends our nation has ever produced.

"Gordie Howe is the greatest player who ever lived; there's not even a question about it."

Those words were spoken by Wayne Gretzky. If anyone would know, it is Gretzky, who himself chose to play in the number 99 to honor the legend known as Mr. Hockey.

When one thinks of Gordie Howe, the first thing that comes to mind is unprecedented longevity. Howe's career began while Harry Truman was president (1946) and finished while Jimmy Carter was in the White House (1980); he made his debut as an eighteen-year-old and finished as a grandfather. During the years in between he played more games, scored more goals, tallied more assists, and totaled more points than any player that came before him. In fact, up to the time of this writing, no player in NHL history—not Gretzky, nor Mario Lemieux, nor anyone else—ever collected more points for any franchise than the 1,809 Howe did for the Detroit Red Wings.

In his NHL debut, Howe finished with one goal and three lost teeth, beginning a career that would see him amass 1,685 minutes—the equivalent of twenty-eight full games—in the penalty box. It was this propensity to mix it up that led to the commonly understood achievement of the "Gordie Howe hat trick"—a goal, an assist, and a fight.

But it is important for younger fans to understand that Howe's brilliance was rooted in much more than just longevity and toughness. His wrist shot was timed at slightly over 114 miles per hour. He finished in the top five in the NHL in scoring in

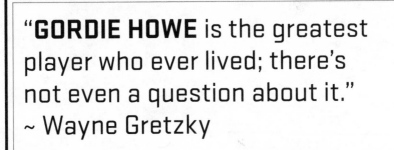

"**GORDIE HOWE** is the greatest player who ever lived; there's not even a question about it." ~ Wayne Gretzky

an unimaginable twenty consecutive seasons. Howe won the Hart Trophy as the league's most valuable player six times and appeared in a record twenty-three all-star games. When Howe retired for the first time, in 1971, his margin as the NHL's all-time leader in points was 590 ahead of Jean Béliveau. He was elected to the Hall of Fame the following year—and then promptly *un*retired. In total, Howe played 499 games and collected 549 points as a Hall of Famer alone.

Fittingly, Mr. Hockey played his greatest seasons in Hockeytown and makes an outstanding case to be the greatest athlete in the history of Detroit sports. Consider that Ty Cobb, Isiah Thomas, and Barry Sanders combined to bring the city two championships; Gordie Howe won four Stanley Cups with the Red Wings. Of his own career, Howe once said, "It would make me very happy to be remembered with respect." That legacy seems certain and secure, and well worthy of his ownership of the number 9 for all time.

Our nation is passionate about sport to be sure, but, for varying reasons, we've not only never embraced soccer in a manner akin to most of the rest of the world, we've never fully recognized the global impact of the game. As a first step toward pointing out how bizarre this blind spot is, I offer the following two illustrations in the life of Brazilian soccer legend Edson Arantes do Nascimento, known to the world as Pelé. First, in 1969, at the height of the tragedy that was the Nigerian Civil War—in which over a million people died—a forty-eight-hour ceasefire was called between the Nigerian government and the secessionist state of Biafra so they could watch Pelé play. Receiving incessant applause and a standing ovation from the fans during the game, Pelé's very presence literally inspired people to cease killing one another. The second illustration of Pelé's profile is a bit more straightforward: In 1970, the soccer legend was named the most famous person in the world, ahead of Neil Armstrong, Elvis Presley, Muhammad Ali, and Pope Paul VI.

It was Pelé himself who coined the phrase "The Beautiful Game," and in its rich history no one has ever played the game nearly as beautifully as he; the list of accomplishments is truly astounding. Pelé is the only player to win three World Cups. At the first of those, in 1958, at the age of seventeen, he became the youngest scorer, youngest hat-trick scorer, youngest final player, and youngest final scorer in World Cup history. He remains the only player under eighteen to score in a World Cup, netting six goals. Further, Pelé was the first player with a

> # At the height of the Nigerian Civil War, a 48-hour ceasefire was called so people could watch **PELÉ** play.

goal at three different World Cups. Brazil outscored its opponents by 23 goals in fourteen World Cup matches with him on the pitch, going 12–1–1 in World Cup matches in which he played, and never losing a match in which he scored. In all, he scored an astronomical 1,281 career goals in 1,363 games, which remains the world record to this day. It is no wonder that when FIFA named its Player of the Century, Pelé received 73 percent of the vote. No other player received more than 10 percent. Pelé was also named the Athlete of the Century by the

International Olympic Committee. In 1999, *Time* magazine released a much-publicized list of the most important people of the century, which included three athletes: Muhammad Ali, Jackie Robinson, and Pelé.

Pelé's jersey number 10 became iconic in every corner of the globe, but only by chance. Brazil forgot to submit its uniform numbers to FIFA for the 1958 World Cup and thus they were chosen randomly. Virtually none of the numbers made positional sense. Pelé—who began that competition as a reserve—somehow received the perfect designation. He then proceeded to make it the most famous number in the glorious history of planet earth's most beautiful and beloved game.

An opposing coach once said of Isiah Lord Thomas, "I call him the baby-faced assassin, because he smiles at you, then cuts you down." Truer words have rarely been spoken—it is hard to recall a player whose appearance more belied his reality. That cherubic face, diminutive stature, and dazzling smile couldn't have been more misleading; few players in basketball history have been tougher or more fiercely competitive than the Detroit Pistons' number 11.

The legend began on the playgrounds of Chicago and then flourished under Bobby Knight at Indiana, where, in 1981, on the same day President Reagan was shot, Thomas led the Hoosiers to a national title, scoring 23 points in the championship game and being named Most Outstanding Player. He was then drafted by the Pistons, who were, in a word, terrible, going 37–127 in the two seasons prior to his arrival. During Thomas's thirteen seasons, the team made the playoffs nine straight years, and Thomas was an all-star in twelve. In my view, the "Bad Boys" Pistons are in fact among the most underappreciated great teams ever, for two reasons. The first is reflected in their nickname; those teams are remembered as much for their brutality as their brilliance. The other factor is purely a function of timing. The decade of the 1980s was dominated by legendary Lakers and Celtics teams, and the '90s was the era of Michael Jordan's Bulls. Sandwiched in between were back-to-back Detroit champions led by a six-foot-one point guard. History is not kind enough to those teams, or to Thomas.

ISIAH THOMAS is the best "little man" in basketball history.

Consider: Isiah Thomas's teams eliminated Michael Jordan from the playoffs three times, Larry Bird twice, and split with Magic Johnson in the finals. In their two championship seasons, the Pistons went 30–7 in the playoffs and eliminated fifteen Hall of Famers along the way, with Thomas leading the team in minutes, points, assists, and steals. However, for me it was actually in defeat that Thomas had his finest hour: In game six of the 1988 NBA Finals against the Lakers, hobbled by a badly sprained ankle, Isiah scored 43 points (essentially on one leg) and added 8 assists and 6 steals in a 103–102 loss. It was a game that no one who watched will ever forget.

I have said ad nauseam across all the platforms I am privileged to host that Isiah Thomas is the best "little man" in basketball history. Your team can have Allen Iverson, Steve Nash, John Stockton, or Chris Paul, and I have no doubt they will be terrific and put up impressive numbers. Nevertheless, I will take Isiah Thomas, and my team will beat your team. Sometimes, it's just as simple as that.

You don't need me to tell you Tom Brady is the greatest quarterback who ever lived. Anyone who has paid even peripheral attention to the sport in the past two decades is very much aware of that. Such is the greatness of Brady that his historical rivals are not even football players—rather they are the other G.O.A.T.s of their respective sports, such as Michael Jordan and Wayne Gretzky. Because of the recency of Brady's career, and the media's breathless documentation of his exploits, you may well believe that you are aware of everything there is to know about him. Well, think again. Below, please find the top twelve things you should (but may not) know about Thomas Edward Patrick Brady Jr., the most accomplished player in the history of pro football, as of the end of the 2021 NFL season.

> #12. In Brady's entire career as a starting quarterback, he never played a game in week ten or later in which his team had a losing record.

#11. Brady was, famously, the 199th pick in the 2000 NFL Draft. There were six quarterbacks taken ahead of him. Of those, only two of them won as many as five games as a starter.

#10. The most accomplished rivals of Brady during his career were, in no particular order: Brett Favre, Peyton Manning, Drew Brees, and Aaron Rodgers. If you add their totals together, that group combined to win two fewer championships than Brady.

#9. In the three Super Bowls Tom Brady lost, he threw 6 touchdowns and 1 interception.

#8. In one of those games, Super Bowl LII against Philadelphia, he set the postseason record with 505 passing yards, was not intercepted, and his team scored 33 points and never punted. It is perfectly reasonable to suggest Brady played well enough to win all ten Super Bowls he played in.

#7. In Super Bowl LI, Brady brought his Patriots back from a 25-point deficit to win. Prior to that comeback, no Super Bowl champion had ever overcome a lead of greater than 10 points.

#6. Brady teamed with Bill Belichick to reach nine Super Bowls as a duo, more than any other *franchise* in NFL history.

#5. Including the playoffs, Brady and Belichick won 249 games together. No other coach-quarterback tandem is within 100 wins of that mark.

#4. Brady won a total of thirty-five postseason games in his career. As of this writing, the only *franchises* with more postseason wins (aside from the Patriots) are the

THOMAS EDWARD
PATRICK BRADY JR.,
THE MOST ACCOMPLISHED PLAYER
IN THE HISTORY OF PRO FOOTBALL.

Packers and Steelers, who were founded in 1921 and 1933 respectively.

#3. Including the playoffs, Brady is 278–85 in his career. Put another way, he won 193 more games than he lost. The only other quarterbacks to even *win* that many games were Peyton Manning and Brett Favre.

#2. Steve Young, Dan Marino, John Elway, Joe Montana, and Otto Graham were all among the greatest quarterbacks ever to play. Each of them was enshrined in the Pro Football Hall of Fame at the age of forty-three. When Brady was forty-three, he was named the MVP of the Super Bowl.

#1. At the time of his first retirement, Brady had won more Super Bowls (seven) than any NFL franchise. (The Patriots and Steelers have each won six, the Cowboys and Niners five.)

And yet, none of these facts, nor even the sum total of all of them, adequately describes the genius of Tom Brady. His leadership, determination, selflessness, and competitiveness are qualities that those of us on the outside are only able to see on Sundays. To hear his former teammates speak of him is to get a more nuanced understanding of Brady's ability as a force multiplier: He genuinely elevated practically everyone around him. We could write about him forever and not do his story justice. Suffice it to say, number 12, Tom Brady, is the greatest football player that has ever lived, and it has been a privilege to witness and chronicle his entire career.

"When Dan Marino was in his prime, he threw the ball better than any quarterback probably who has ever played the game." Jimmy Johnson, the Hall of Fame coach and legendary commentator, said that.

I, meanwhile, would respectfully quarrel only with the word "probably." I have seen all the great quarterbacks dating back to the 1970s, and I would argue that none of them ever threw the football as well as the guy who wore number 13 in Miami.

Dan Marino's "golden arm" first became the stuff of legend at Pitt, where he was 33–3 through his junior season. He then proceeded to throw 23 interceptions against only 17 touchdowns as a senior, and that, combined with wholly unsubstantiated rumors of Marino being of questionable character, caused him to become the sixth quarterback selected in the first round of the 1983 NFL Draft—the most famous and accomplished quarterback class of all time. Proving in the NFL that his senior year was a fluke, his extraordinary talent almost instantly lifted Marino to superstardom. In 1984, his second season, he had arguably the greatest year of any quarterback that ever lived. His 5,084 yards that season not only set a record but hit a benchmark many had previously thought unattainable; it was not until 2008 that Drew Brees became the second QB ever to throw for 5,000 yards. Marino also threw 48 touchdowns in 1984; the previous record had been 36. *That* mark stood until 2004. For further context, consider Marino accounted for 7.8 percent of the league total in touchdown passes that legendary season—in 2020, that would have equated to throwing 67 touchdowns. At

No quarterback has ever thrown the football better than the guy who wore **NUMBER 13** in Miami.

twenty-three years of age, Marino was the youngest quarterback ever to be named MVP, and remains as of this writing the youngest quarterback to ever start a Super Bowl.

Perhaps the most famous game Marino ever played was against the Chicago Bears on a Monday night during the 1985 season. The Bears that season had what many (including me) believe was the greatest defense of all time. Consider, in their other eighteen games (including the playoffs) Chicago allowed fewer than 10 points per game, giving up just 14 touchdown passes while intercepting 36 passes. In the three games directly leading up to their showdown with the Dolphins, the Bears allowed a *combined* total of 3 points. Marino then went and put up 38 against them, three touchdowns and just one pick; it was the only game the Bears would lose all year.

Unfortunately for Marino, while most of his records have fallen, he remains at the very top of one unfortunate list: the greatest players to never win a championship. "I'd trade every record we broke to be Super Bowl champs," he has said. Indeed, his legacy is partially clouded by his 8–10 postseason record, though it is worthy of note that the Miami defenses allowed 345 points in those ten defeats. Regardless, it is impossible to have watched Dan Marino throw a football and not be forever changed by the experience. He may not have always been lucky, but the number 13 is his until the end of time.

There are a great many things in the history of sports that I cannot prove yet know for absolute certain all the same, and at the very top of that list is this: There has never been a baseball player who loved to play the game more than Peter Edward Rose.

Generations of fans who did not see him play, and thus know him only as the cartoonish outcast he has become, are forgiven for having no idea why the rest of us care so deeply about his lifelong battle with the sport and his candidacy for the Hall of Fame. Very simply, it comes down to this: Pete Rose played baseball with all the passion and joy we dreamed we would if only we'd been good enough to make it to The Show ourselves. It is ironic that a man banished for life for breaking the most important rule in sports was once best known for never, ever cheating the game.

"Charlie Hustle" was his nickname, and it was well-earned, partly derived from his famous insistence on sprinting to first base whenever he would draw a walk, something Little Leaguers have now done for half a century because of him. It is reasonable, I believe, to assume that no player has ever been pointed to more frequently by parents and coaches as the ultimate example of How to Play the Game than number 14 for the Cincinnati Reds.

What should not be lost beneath those intangibles, however, is just how great a ballplayer Pete Rose was. He remains, as of this writing—and very likely will as long as the game is played—the all-time leader in hits, singles, times reaching base, plate appearances, and games played. He was the leadoff hitter for

> There has never been a baseball player who loved to play the game more than **PETE ROSE**.

the Big Red Machine, Cincinnati's back-to-back championship teams in 1975 and '76, and led the majors in runs scored both of those seasons. He was MVP of the '75 World Series, perhaps the most dramatic ever played. In all, he played on six teams that reached the World Series, winning three, and was an all-star seventeen times at five different positions.

Throughout much of the early part of my radio career, if I ever encountered a slow news day in sports, there was no easier solution than throwing open the phone lines and asking listeners: "Should Pete Rose be in the Hall of Fame?" No player I am aware of stirred as much emotion among fans of sport. As for me, I have long said I believe Rose belongs in Cooperstown. His lifetime ban from the game is well-earned and fair punishment for his misdeeds—he should never be allowed to earn a living from the game again, and he will not. However, the memories he created and his greatness as a player deserve to be memorialized. The Hall of Fame is not solely for the Hall of Famers—it is for the rest of us, too. For all his unforgivable behavior and dishonesty, his place in the fabric of the game's history is too substantial to be forgotten or ignored.

There is a very legitimate case to be made that Tim Tebow is the greatest college quarterback that ever lived. The larger-than-life nature of his celebrity, coupled with his complicated tenure as a professional, have somewhat obscured his exploits at the University of Florida. But make no mistake: As a collegian, Tebow was as accomplished as any player ever, and it is *that* jersey number 15, and that legacy, that is enshrined here.

As a freshman, in 2006, Tebow produced 13 touchdowns on a Gators team that won the national championship. The following season, Tebow became the full-time starter and created an SEC record 55 touchdowns, becoming the first underclassman ever to win the Heisman Trophy. During his junior season, Tebow added 42 more touchdowns, finishing third in the Heisman voting and leading the Gators to another national title. His senior year, Tebow produced 35 touchdowns and led Florida to a 13–1 finish. In all, Tebow's teams went 35–6 when he started at quarterback, averaging 41 points and 453 yards per game. He was the first quarterback to finish in the top five of Heisman voting in three different seasons. His 3,922 Heisman voting points remain the most for any quarterback ever.

Tebow's achievements were not only memorable, they were also unprecedented. His 55 touchdowns in 2007 were *14 more* than any SEC player had ever scored before. His 145 career touchdowns remain a conference record to this day. His 23 rushing touchdowns during his Heisman season were also record setting; consider that conference immortals Herschel Walker, Bo Jackson, and Emmitt Smith never scored as many

> There is a very legitimate case to be made that **TIM TEBOW** is the greatest college quarterback that ever lived.

as 20. In one stretch, Tebow recorded at least one passing and rushing touchdown in fourteen consecutive games, something no other player has ever done in the history of major college football.

With Tim Tebow, however, it has never been solely about *what* he did, but also about the way he did it. The fiery passion and leadership he displayed went as far toward making him a legend as all the exploits we've just detailed. That piece of his legacy can best be illustrated by Tebow himself. In 2008, after a disappointing September defeat, the junior quarterback addressed the assembled media and made what is perhaps the most famous speech ever given by a college football player:

> *To the fans and everybody in Gator Nation, I'm sorry, extremely sorry. We were hoping for an undefeated season. That was my goal, something Florida's never done here. But I promise you one thing, a lot of good will come out of this. You will never see any player in the entire country play as hard as I will play the rest of the season, and you will never see someone push the rest of the team as hard as I will push everybody the rest of the season, and you will never see a team play harder than we will the rest of the season. God bless.*

That promise, delivered with tears in his eyes, was one Tim Tebow kept. He led his team to a national championship that season. Today those words are engraved on a plaque outside the entrance to the team's football facility. Inside the stadium, there is a statue of the man who spoke them. And in this book, there is a place for his jersey; the number 15 belongs to him.

"I don't ever see myself like him. He was so spectacular, I think he's in a league of his own. Every time he took the field, it felt like he was going to win." Believe it or not, those words were not spoken about Tom Brady, they were spoken *by* him when asked about his childhood idol, the great Joe Montana.

When Brady was a boy in Northern California, it was Joe Cool who first made him love football, and when Brady finally did ascend and become the greatest quarterback of all time, it was Montana he surpassed.

Joe Montana was a legend before he became a superstar. Leading Notre Dame to the national title in 1977, he remains as of this writing the most recent quarterback to win both a college national championship and a Super Bowl. (Joe Namath was the only other.) Montana was drafted in the third round by San Francisco, where he ultimately teamed with head coach Bill Walsh to form one of the most perfect unions in the history of

American sports. It could be argued, in fact, that no quarterback ever had a decade that remotely compared to Montana's from 1981 through 1990. During those ten seasons, Montana went 112–38, including the playoffs, winning two regular season MVPs, three Super Bowl MVPs, and four Super Bowl titles. Drilling down further, Montana's absolute apex may well have been the highest in history: In the calendar years 1989 and 1990, he went 31–3, winning six playoff games by a combined 154 points, and capturing two Super Bowl trophies.

Those are a lot of numbers, of course, and spectacular they certainly are, but to have watched Joe Montana play is to know that his flair for the dramatic and his ability to raise his level in

JOE MONTANA was a legend before he became a superstar.

the grandest moments were actually the most important parts of his legacy. That story begins in earnest in January 1982, with perhaps the most famous pass in football history, the touchdown he threw to Dwight Clark to win the NFC Championship game en route to his first Super Bowl title, a play forever known simply as The Catch. He then bookended his magical decade with two more titles: one of them ending in a 92-yard drive in the final minute, culminating in a game-winning touchdown pass to John Taylor, the other representing the most lopsided win in Super Bowl history. In all, he finished a perfect 4–0 in Super Bowls, his team averaging 34.8 points. Montana threw

11 touchdowns against 0 interceptions in those four games; his passer rating of 127.8 remains the highest in Super Bowl history, and his sixteen playoff victories were the most all-time when he retired.

Joe Montana finished his career with two successful seasons in Kansas City, wearing the jersey number 19 and leading the Chiefs to within a game of the 1993 Super Bowl. But it is not in that uniform that he will be forever remembered. Montana's mythical run in San Francisco was as compelling, brilliant, and flat-out epic as any the game of football has ever seen. In a crowded and spectacularly accomplished field, he is the easy choice for number 16.

The arguments over the greatest player ever in any given sport are always, for obvious reasons, the most fervid we have. Conversely, the arguments over the most underappreciated tend to be the most tepid, for equally obvious reasons. That said, I would posit that John Havlicek is the most underappreciated immortal we have in American sports history. As proof, I offer all of the following, most of which will come as a shock to all but the most astute fans; the fact that you very likely will be taken aback by the magnitude of what you are about to read is my point exactly.

To begin, number 17 scored more points in a Celtics uniform than anyone who ever lived—more than Bill Russell, more than Larry Bird. In fact, at the time of Havlicek's retirement he ranked third all-time in league scoring, behind only Wilt Chamberlain and Oscar Robertson. Havlicek was also sixth all-time in assists, which speaks to his practically unprecedented impact on every element of the game; as of this writing, there are only two players in history who amassed 26,000 points, 8,000 rebounds, and 6,000 assists in their careers: LeBron James and John Havlicek. (Notably, one of those two played his entire career prior to the advent of the three-point shot.) Further, "Hondo" was named to the NBA's all-defensive team eight times, which is fitting when you consider he made the most famous defensive play in the history of the sport: intercepting Hal Greer's inbounds pass to preserve a one-point Celtics victory in game seven of the Eastern Finals in 1965, a play immortalized by Johnny Most's call of "Havlicek stole the ball!"

> **JOHN HAVLICEK** is the most underappreciated immortal in American sports history.

In all, Havlicek's teams won eight championships, and he was the leading scorer on four of them. Perhaps his most extraordinary attribute was his durability: During his sixteen seasons, Havlicek's Celtics played 1,481 games (including the playoffs) and Havlicek played in 1,442 of them; he missed thirty-nine games in sixteen seasons. All this success came on the heels of one of the greatest careers in collegiate basketball history: His Ohio State teams were 78–6 during his three seasons, and he led the Buckeyes to the national title game all three years.

If history has failed to give Havlicek his due, the men he

played with, and for, cannot be blamed. The respect he engendered during his career has indeed proved undying.

"The best all-around player I ever saw," said Bill Russell.

"The greatest basketball player who ever lived, bar none," said Bobby Knight.

Perhaps the greatest praise of all came from the greatest judge of talent in the history of the game. "There isn't anything on a basketball court he can't do," Red Auerbach once said. "John Havlicek is what I always thought a Celtic should be."

Okay, so now you're going to be mad at me.

And I get it.

Peyton Manning is one of my favorite players too, and one of the greatest quarterbacks that ever lived. But, Jack Nicklaus is the greatest, and most accomplished, human being to ever play the great game of golf, and with his 18 major championships, 18 is the number with which he will forever be associated.

Unless Tiger Woods magically discovers the Fountain of Youth, there is no player currently on the PGA Tour who will ever so much as *threaten* to win that many major championships—in fact, I would confidently wager that Jack's record for majors will survive as long as any career record in any sport. He deserves a place in this collection, despite not having a uniform number to represent. 18 is Jack's number—it belongs to him.

An argument could be made that the Golden Bear was as good in the biggest events as any player has ever been in any sport. Consider: He won as many Masters, US Opens, and PGA Championships as any player that ever lived. Further, in a sport where second place is far more than just the "first loser," his record 19 second-place finishes at majors are nearly as revered as his 18 wins. In a stretch of 39 consecutive majors, from the 1969 Masters through the 1978 Open Championship, he didn't miss a single cut. In all, he finished in the top ten at 73 major championships; Sam Snead is next on the list with 48. Nicklaus carded 218 rounds under par at majors; at the time of his last such round that was 67 more than any player in history.

> # JACK NICKLAUS's record for majors wins will survive as long as any career record in any sport.

Jack won his first major at the age of twenty-two and achieved the career Grand Slam at twenty-six. He won at least one tour event in each of seventeen straight years, a record he shares with his lifelong friend and rival Arnold Palmer. He won his last major in 1986 at Augusta, shooting 65 on perhaps the most famous Sunday in Masters history. For as long as the game is played, golfers will shout, "Yes sir!" when they roll in clutch putts, as Verne Lundquist legendarily did when Jack made birdie on seventeen. The twenty-four-year gap between Nicklaus's first major and his last is the longest in the history of golf.

The brilliant columnist Thomas Boswell perhaps summed it up best, with words that could be used to describe Jack's entire career every bit as much as its most famous triumph. "Some things cannot possibly happen," Boswell wrote, "because they are both too improbable and too perfect. The US hockey team cannot beat the Russians in the 1980 Olympics. Jack Nicklaus cannot shoot 65 to win the Masters at age forty-six. Nothing else comes immediately to mind."

Perhaps the easiest sports question one could ask today is: Who is the greatest quarterback of all time? In fact, it isn't even worth asking—Tom Brady has so distanced himself from the field as to render the discussion uninteresting.

However, there was a time when that same question was just as easy to answer, but the answer was John Constantine Unitas, number 19 for the Baltimore Colts.

There is perhaps no greater rags-to-riches story in NFL history. Consider that when Unitas was cut by the Steelers during his first training camp in 1955, he hitchhiked home and spent the season playing semipro ball for six dollars per game while working as a pile driver at a construction site. By the time he retired after the 1973 season, number 19 held twenty-two NFL records, including most passing yards and passing touchdowns. He was the first quarterback to win 100 games. He once threw at least one touchdown in forty-seven consecutive games, a record that stood until Drew Brees broke it in 2012, though Unitas remains the only quarterback to lead the league in touchdown passes in four straight seasons.

The legend of Johnny U was born, in earnest, in the most famous football game ever played, the 1958 NFL Championship Game at Yankee Stadium, in which Unitas's Colts beat the Giants. There were twelve Hall of Famers on the field that day. Unitas led Baltimore on an eighty-yard drive to win in the first sudden-death overtime in pro football history. When the league celebrated its centennial in 2020, that game was voted the greatest ever played. Further, when the league celebrated

> There is perhaps no greater rags-to-riches story in NFL history than that of **JOHNNY UNITAS**.

its eightieth anniversary in the year 2000, the Hall of Fame selection committee named Unitas the greatest quarterback ever to play.

There are other ties that bind the former G.O.A.T. to the current one: As of this writing, Unitas and Brady are the only players ever with at least three MVP awards and three championships. While Brady is revered by teammates, legendary tight end John Mackey once said of Unitas, "It was like being in a huddle with God."

And, as with Brady, athletic gifts were not what separated Unitas from the pack. "What made him the greatest quarterback of all time wasn't his arm or his size, it was what was inside his stomach," said Ernie Accorsi, who was an executive in the league for more than thirty years. "If I had my career on the line for one drive, after all the football I've seen in my life, John Unitas would be the guy I want."

I fell in love with football sometime in the early 1970s, which means as of this writing I have been obsessed with the sport for nearly fifty years. If you asked me to name the single most exciting player I've watched during this nearly half a century—the one most worth the price of admission—with no hesitation whatsoever I would tell you it was Barry Sanders.

I could, and will, go through a litany of numbers that illustrate Sanders's greatness, but to be very clear, no illustration could ever do justice to the sheer joy of watching the man run. I am fully comfortable positing that no player in the game's history ever made more defenders fall down in hopeless pursuit of a tackle. Barry Sanders was electric; there was never a single play in which he was not a threat to score a touchdown.

The numbers, meanwhile, are indeed ridiculous. Sanders is the only player ever to rush for at least 1,100 yards in ten straight seasons, and they were the only ten seasons he played.

He rushed for at least 100 in fourteen straight games in 1997, still the longest streak in NFL history. Sanders averaged 1,527 rushing yards per season, the most ever by a wide margin. Sanders had 27 rushing touchdowns of at least 25 yards, the most all-time. He had twenty-five games of at least 150 yards rushing, the most ever. When he retired abruptly after the 1998 season, he was fewer than 1,500 yards from Walter Payton's career rushing record, a mark he almost certainly would have broken had he continued even one more year.

Meanwhile, no immortal in the history of the sport was ever a greater victim of organizational ineptitude than number 20. The Detroit Lions have won *one* playoff game since winning the NFL championship in 1957; that was in 1991, when they

> # BARRY SANDERS was a once-in-a-lifetime talent.

won a franchise-best twelve games behind a league-high 17 touchdowns from Sanders. During his ten seasons in Detroit, the Lions started ten different quarterbacks. Even so, Sanders led them to the postseason five times between 1991 and 1997— they've only been back four times since his retirement. Simply put, the Lions have been a football laughingstock for generations, and Sanders was a victim of that circumstance.

At five foot eight, Barry Sanders is the shortest player in the Pro Football Hall of Fame. He had stunningly powerful legs, routinely squatting 600 pounds, roughly three times his body weight. He once juked fellow Hall of Famer Rod Woodson so mercilessly that Woodson tore an ACL on the play. Sanders was a once-in-a-lifetime talent. For my money, there has never been a superstar who was more thrilling to watch in the history of his sport.

"Any time you have an opportunity to make a difference in this world and you don't, then you are wasting your time on earth."

So said Pittsburgh Pirates number 21, Roberto Clemente, a man who tried to do as much good for humanity as any athlete that ever lived. Today one of the most prized Major League Baseball awards bears his name: The Roberto Clemente Award is presented annually to the player who demonstrates the values this Hall of Famer displayed in his commitment to sportsmanship, community, and helping others. Both on and off the field, Clemente was an icon.

As time has passed, and the spotlight on Clemente's philanthropy and his impact on Latin American baseball have reached mythical stature, what is perhaps lost is just how special a *player* he was. The Great One reached 3,000 hits in what proved to be his final at-bat, the first player born outside the United States to reach that plateau. He won four batting titles—as many as

BOTH ON AND OFF THE FIELD,

ROBERTO CLEMENTE

WAS AN ICON.

his contemporaries Hank Aaron, Frank Robinson, and Willie Mays combined. Clemente also won twelve Gold Gloves, tied with Mays for the most ever as an outfielder. And he was so special that the Hall of Fame waived its mandatory waiting period, allowing him to be voted in less than one year after his tragic death in a plane crash.

In fairness, though, to acknowledge only Clemente's play would be to capture way less than half of his impact on the game. Major League Baseball is today made up of around 25 percent Latin American players. Roberto Clemente deserves more credit for that than any person who ever lived.

"For me, he is the Jackie Robinson of Latin baseball," said former big league player and manager Ozzie Guillen, a native of Venezuela. "He lived racism. He was a man who was happy to be not only Puerto Rican, but Latin American. He let people know that. And that is something that is very important for all of us."

Clemente faced racism, as well as a language barrier and a condescending press that often quoted him in broken English with derisively phonetic spelling. None of that diminished his humanity and compassion; Clemente visited patients at Pittsburgh's Children's Hospital during the season, staged free baseball clinics for low-income children in Puerto Rico, and continued playing winter ball well past the time that he needed to because he felt an obligation to the people of his homeland, who otherwise would not have a chance to see him play. He died when the plane he was in went down as he was en route to delivering earthquake-relief supplies in Nicaragua. He did not have to get on that plane, but he felt it was important to do so, given reports that the Nicaraguan military was stealing relief supplies and selling them for profit. Clemente believed that if he was on board, given his celebrity status, the chances of the relief supplies being intercepted would be lessened. Roberto Clemente was thirty-eight years old when he died as he lived, making a profound impact upon the world that to this day extends well beyond the genius of his play.

The Dallas Cowboys of the 1990s were such a collection of stars that at times they felt more like a constellation than a football team. Their rugged, handsome quarterback is in the Hall of Fame, as is the outlandish wide receiver and the genius head coach who put all the stars into those star-covered helmets. But none of them, not Troy Aikman, nor Michael Irvin, nor even Jimmy Johnson, was the engine of the dynasty in Dallas. The most important person was the classy, comparatively unassuming running back Emmitt Smith. Even the owner, Jerry Jones, who always brings the bombast, acknowledged as much when he said that Smith was "as much a part of the Cowboys as the star."

Those Cowboys became the first team ever to win the Super Bowl three times in a four-year span; Smith led the NFL in rushing all three of those seasons. Terrell Davis is the only other rushing champion ever to win the Super Bowl. In 1993, Smith may have had the greatest season of any running back ever: He led the NFL in rushing yards and yards from scrimmage, and was named MVP of the league and Super Bowl MVP. He remains the only running back ever to win MVP and the Super Bowl in the same year. During six consecutive seasons in which the Cowboys made the playoffs (1991–96), Smith rushed for 115 touchdowns. Barry Sanders and Ricky Watters, who ranked second and third respectively, *combined* for 115. In all, Smith rushed for 1,586 yards and 19 touchdowns in the postseason, both records that still stand, as does the five rushing touchdowns he registered in Super Bowls.

EMMITT SMITH was "as much a part of the Cowboys as the star." ~ Jerry Jones

Emmitt Smith's durability may be every bit as legendary as his productivity. Consider: There have only been four seasons in NFL history in which a player had 500 touches. Smith accounted for two of those, early in his career, but still played in 218 of a possible 225 games as a Cowboy, with two of the seven he missed being the result of a contract holdout. He maintains the career record for most touches by a wide margin—787 more than Walter Payton. It was, of course, Payton's career rushing-yards record that he famously broke; Smith finished with 18,355, a mark that may never be approached, considering the modern emphasis on passing and multiple back schemes.

Smith wore the same jersey number 22 in college, where he averaged 126.7 rushing yards per game at Florida, still second-most in SEC history behind only Herschel Walker. But it was in the NFL that Emmitt Smith took hold of 22, as the greatest player on one of the greatest teams in pro football history.

"Had Emmitt gone down, there was no plan B," said Troy Aikman. "It was just Emmitt."

23

If there is one thing for which I have been m[ost ridi]culed during my time at ESPN, it is the frequenc[y with which] I mention that I began my career covering Mi[chael Jordan] and the Chicago Bulls. In response to this criti[cism, I] ask: If *you* had been fortunate enough to occupy [the] piano bench while Mozart tickled the keys, or if [you held the] smock in the studio while Picasso painted a can[vas, wouldn't] *you* talk about it a lot? For the record, I do not co[nsider either] of those comparisons to be overreaching. For nea[rly a decade,] I had the privilege of a front-row seat to the gre[atest of] the history of sports. Any day that I do *not* menti[on it, I show] enormous restraint.

My most lasting recollection of that time, mor[e than] the titles or Olympics or commercials, was the e[xtreme] intensity with which Jordan competed every sing[le night. It] seems especially noteworthy in this era when he[…]

MICHAEL JORDAN

WAS ABSOLUTELY EVERYTHING YOU COULD
EVER WISH AN ATHLETE TO BE.

routinely sit out games in the interest of "load management," their actions openly stating that some games aren't all that important to them. In Michael Jordan's final three seasons in Chicago, he did not miss a single game, and he approached a Tuesday night matchup with New Jersey in February with the same tenacity he displayed in the playoffs. This dedication remains my favorite piece of his legacy, and it manifested itself foremostly on the defensive end of the floor. Consider that there have been eleven seasons in NBA history where a player scored 2,000 points and recorded 200 steals, and Michael Jordan is responsible for six of them. He won ten scoring titles (the most ever) and was named first-team all-defense nine times (tied for the most ever). He remains the only player ever to win Defensive Player of the Year and lead the league in scoring in the same season.

Meanwhile, Jordan's offensive accomplishments are thoroughly mind-blowing. He is the all-time leader in points per game in the regular season *and* the postseason. He once scored in double figures for a record 1,041 consecutive games, which is 366 games longer than the number two player in history. He played in thirty-seven playoff series and led both teams in scoring in thirty-six of them. He had five career playoff games with at least 55 points; no other player has more than one. He averaged 30 points in the playoffs in twelve different seasons; Jerry West is next on that list with seven. Since the advent of the three-point line, Jordan is the only player to average 35 points in a season more than once.

More than anything, though, Michael Jordan is known for winning. The game-winning jumper to claim the NCAA title for North Carolina—as a freshman. Two Olympic gold medals.

And, of course, six NBA championships, a perfect six-for-six in the finals, the most wins in the championship round without a loss by an MVP in NBA, NHL, MLB, or NFL history. He was the MVP in all six of those finals, to go along with his five regular season MVPs. But, again, Michael cared about winning every time he set foot on the court, not just when the title was at stake. In November 1990, his team lost three straight games—it would not lose three in a row ever again while he was in Chicago. In all, Jordan went 631 games between three-game losing streaks.

Simply put, Michael Jeffrey Jordan was absolutely everything you could ever wish an athlete to be. He cared about the fans, he was endlessly accommodating to the media, and he cared more about winning than he did anything else, including money. The lessons I learned just being in his orbit have served me well. He was the best player ever, in his or any sport. If there were only space for one athlete in this book, it would be him.

"If somebody came up and hit .450, stole 100 bases and per-
formed a miracle in the field every day, I'd still look you in the
eye and say, 'Willie Mays was better.'"

Leo Durocher, who played twenty years of Major League
Baseball and then won over 2,000 games as a manager, said
that. It seems fitting that a man nicknamed Leo the Lip would
find such a creative way to convey what I will put much more
simply here: We have been playing the game of baseball for
roughly 150 years, and in that time, the best ever to play it was
Willie Howard Mays Jr. There wasn't anything on the field
number 24 couldn't do. In fact, not only could he do *everything*
at an elite level, he did everything as well as practically anyone
ever did anything. For example, Mays led his league in home
runs and steals four times each, the only player in history to
do that. He led the majors in steals in the decade of the 1950s,
and in home runs for the '50s and '60s with a total of 600—an

unprecedented combination of offensive power and speed. Meanwhile, he was also inarguably the greatest outfielder in the history of the game: Mays recorded 7,112 putouts, a record that will never be broken. He won twelve Gold Glove awards in a row from 1957 through 1968, while during that time also hitting 435 home runs. That combination of genius at the plate, on the basepaths, and in the field has never been replicated.

With Mays, however, as with all the great ones, the memories are more about the moments than they are the numbers. He homered for his very first career hit, off the Hall of Famer Warren Spahn, causing Spahn to say, "I'll never forgive myself.

> We have been playing the game of baseball for roughly 150 years, and in that time, the best ever to play it was **WILLIE HOWARD MAYS JR**.

We might have gotten rid of Willie forever if I'd only struck him out." Mays made the most famous catch in the history of the sport, forever known simply as The Catch, in game one of the 1954 World Series. The ball was hit by Vic Wertz and traveled 460 feet to center field in the Polo Grounds. The chase-down catch was not merely spectacular, it was critical, preserving a 2–2 tie in a game that Mays's Giants would ultimately win 5–2 en route to sweeping the series. It was the last title the Giants would win in New York; the franchise would not win another until 2010.

On the occasion of Mays's ninetieth birthday, in May 2021, the legendary announcer Vin Scully posted a message on Twitter. "Willie Mays has always been my favorite player, and I've seen a few." Such was the stature of Mays that the voice of the Dodgers—the ultimate archrivals to the Giants—couldn't withhold his admiration. A fitting tribute to the man known as "The Say Hey Kid," the greatest baseball player that ever lived.

There was a time in American society when the dominant sporting figure in the nation was the heavyweight boxing champion of the world, and for a dozen years, from 1937 to 1949, that man was Joe Louis. The undisputed king of boxing's golden age, Louis lays claim to the number 25 on this list for his 25 consecutive title defenses, which remains to this day the most of any heavyweight champion all-time. He won twenty-three title fights by knockout, another record that still stands for any weight class or division. Further, he knocked out six of those opponents in the first round, twice as many as any other boxer.

Louis, the son of an Alabama sharecropper and the great-grandson of slaves, became the youngest-ever heavyweight champion at age twenty-three in 1937, and as such became one of the first African Americans to achieve lasting fame and popularity in the twentieth century. He had been

THE UNDISPUTED KING OF BOXING'S GOLDEN AGE:

JOE LOUIS.

heavyweight champion for a full decade when Jackie Robinson played his first game for the Dodgers. "What my father did was enable white America to think of him as an American, not as a Black," declared his son, Joe Louis Jr. "By winning, he became white America's first Black hero."

The most famous fight of Louis's career, and perhaps one as consequential as any ever contested, came on June 22, 1938, in a rematch against German heavyweight Max Schmeling. Adolf Hitler presented Schmeling as an exemplary representative of the Aryan race. The two men fought in front of more than 70,000 fans at Yankee Stadium, and when Louis knocked out Schmeling in two minutes and four seconds the victory was widely painted as democracy triumphing over fascism. Schmeling spent ten days in a New York hospital after the fight, then six more weeks in a German hospital after that. Historian Bert Sugar described the fight as "The greatest sporting event of the twentieth century."

Joe Louis became an American hero for that victory, and then further endeared himself by announcing that America would win World War II "because we're on God's side." As the war raged on, Louis donated almost a hundred thousand dollars' worth of his earnings to army and navy relief societies. He joined the army himself in 1942, and was part of nearly one hundred boxing exhibitions, performing for over two million members of the military. Forever known as the Brown Bomber, Louis remains among the most iconic figures in the history of American sports.

Owing to the times in which he lived, Louis was often described as a credit to his race. The legendary sportswriter Jimmy Cannon wrote perhaps the perfect response to that notion: "Yes, he is a credit to his race—the human race."

The long-distance race known as a marathon was inspired by the legend of the ancient Greek messenger from 490 BC who raced from the site of Marathon to Athens with news of an important military victory. After making his announcement, the exhausted messenger collapsed and died. In the two and a half millennia that have passed since, the 26.2 mile race has become an integral piece of the fabric of human athletics, and no one has ever run it better than Eliud Kipchoge.

No Human Is Limited is the personal motto of the five-foot-six, 115-pound legend from Kenya; it is also the title of his memoir. Those words were the hashtag that went viral when Kipchoge boldly went where no human had ever gone before, a place that seemed impossible: the sub-two-hour marathon. Imagine running a 100-meter sprint in seventeen seconds, then doing it again, 422 times in succession. That's what it takes to run a marathon in under two hours. The day Kipchoge did it, in

Vienna in 2019, his average mile was run in 4:34. The finishing time of 1:59:40, while considered unofficial, was comparable in magnitude to Roger Bannister running a four-minute mile in 1954. On October 12, 2019, a crowd of 120,000 spectators turned out to watch Kipchoge race, with nearly 5 million viewers on YouTube, and, never one to disappoint, Eliud Kipchoge redefined what the human body is capable of.

Kipchoge grew up in Kapsisiywa, a small village in Nandi County, Kenya. His mother worked as a teacher; his father died when Eliud was young. As he developed as a runner, Kipchoge adopted the habit of smiling whenever pain set in. "Pain," he

> In the two and a half millennia since the **26.2** mile race has become an integral piece of the fabric of human athletics, no one has ever run it better than **ELIUD KIPCHOGE**.

would say, "is nothing more than a mindset." Meanwhile, his talents brought him worldwide renown long before he broke the two-hour barrier. Kipchoge owns four of the top five official marathon times in history, and once ran off an extraordinary streak of ten consecutive marathon wins over a seven-year period. As of this writing, he has run thirteen marathons in

2:05 or faster, five more than any runner in history, and he is one of only three men ever to win two Olympic gold medals in the event.

The belief that no human is limited is far more than just a catchphrase to Kipchoge, who takes great pride in having inspired millions of people across the world. "The reason for running 1:59 is not the performance," he says. "The reason to run 1:59 is to tell that farmer that he is not limited; that teacher that she can produce good results in school; that engineer . . . that he can go to another project." Years of success has brought Kipchoge international admiration and great wealth, though he is clear that those are not his primary motivators. "It's the love of sport and working hard," Kipchoge says. "That's the only thing that is sacred in this world."

ou that the second coming of Mickey Mantle
ıying baseball even as we speak? I might also
e sporting public has responded to this miracle
e yawn.

rtening certainty that a huge swath of today's
e more aware of the exploits of Mantle, who
game more than half a century ago, than those
son Trout. And they should know Trout, if they
about the game at all, because if you strip away
rs, he is the best player the sport has seen in

as twenty years old in his first full season in the
cade that followed may have constituted the
any player ever had. Trout scored more runs in
an Pete Rose, hit more home runs than Willie
more bases than Derek Jeter. He won three MVP

awards in his twenties, his third coming at age twenty-eight, the youngest player in American League history to win three times. Trout is the fastest player ever to amass 300 home runs and 200 steals, reaching those plateaus in sixty fewer games than Mays, who is second. Trout finished in the top five of American League MVP voting in each of his first nine seasons, tied for the most all-time with Mantle and Ted Williams, and Trout did it before turning thirty. The most important statistic in baseball is WAR, Wins Above Replacement. According to that measurement, Trout was the best position player in the AL in five consecutive seasons. Mantle and Babe Ruth are the only other players ever to do that.

MICHAEL TROUT may have been the best twentysomething player ever.

So, that is the historical company Mike Trout keeps, his name continually finding itself situated beside Mantle, Mays, Ruth, and Williams at the absolute apex of the baseball mountain. The conundrum, then, is why all those older names still reverberate more greatly than his while he remains still playing, and in his prime. Part of it is a complete lack of team success. As of this writing, Trout has played his entire career with the Angels, yet has appeared in a total of three playoff games, losing them all. Otherwise put, he has as many MVP awards as he has games of postseason experience. Those games were played in 2014.

Four years later, Mike Trout's Q Score was measured as 22, which basically meant that one in five Americans knew who he was. That survey found the NBA player most comparable to Trout, in terms of societal recognition, was Kenneth Faried.

One way to consider this is: If it doesn't bother Trout, perhaps it shouldn't bother me. It isn't his job to carry the entirety of baseball. His job is to play it to the best of his ability, and he certainly does that. Not everyone is meant to be Michael Jordan. Believe it or not, many people wouldn't even want to be. However you choose to look at that, Trout's brilliance should not be overlooked by those of us who truly care about the sport. His career is hopefully nowhere near complete, but he is already well deserving of a permanent place in the history of sports. 27 belongs to him.

Michael Phelps was born to swim. Quite literally, in fact: When experts talk about the perfect swimmer's body it is *his* that they have in mind. Phelps, at six foot four, has an eighty-inch wingspan, extremely long for a man of his size, and yet he has comparatively short legs, generating less drag for him in the pool. He has oversize hands and feet, which act almost as fins in the water. Those gifts gave the Baltimore Bullet the opportunity to become what he ultimately was meant to be: the most dominant individual athlete in any sport, ever.

Phelps receives ownership of 28 here because of the total number of Olympic medals he won—the most decorated Olympian in history. Twenty-three of those medals were gold; no other Olympian has more than nine. Phelps has more gold medals than any two Olympians combined, ever. Phelps was, and remains, the only athlete ever to win four golds at more than one Olympic games, a feat he accomplished four times.

Michael Phelps burst onto the scene at the Sydney Olympics in 2000 at the age of fifteen, the youngest American man on the Olympic swim team in sixty-eight years. In 2001, still only fifteen years old, he set his first world record, in the 200-meter butterfly. In all, Phelps would break thirty-nine world records between 2001 and 2009, the most of any male swimmer all-time. His consistency of performance boggles the mind: From 2004 through 2016, Phelps medaled in every Olympic event in which he competed, save one, which was a fourth-place finish in the 400-meter individual medley at the 2012 London Games. Phelps won the 200-meter individual medley at four

> # MICHAEL PHELPS is the most dominant individual athlete in any sport, ever.

consecutive Olympics, the first Olympian to win any event four times since Carl Lewis in the long jump. Phelps also won the 100-meter butterfly in three straight Olympic games.

One could easily make the argument that no athlete has ever dominated any sport at any time to the degree that Phelps did at the 2008 Olympics in Beijing. He entered eight events and won them all, setting world records in seven of them. It was the largest haul of medals for any athlete at any Olympic games, and it cemented Michael Phelps's place as not only the greatest ever in his sport, but absolutely on the shortest possible list of the most accomplished athletes our nation has ever produced.

They say that records are made to be broken. Eric Dickerson, the most ebullient, dominating, breathtaking running back of his era, begs to differ. From the instant he veritably burst into the NFL, it was clear he was unlike anything anyone had ever seen. The oversize shoulder pads, the neck roll, the goggles, the upright running style of number 29—it was as though they had handed the football to a sprinter—and sprint he did, as well as anyone in the history of the game.

Dickerson rushed for 1,808 yards as a rookie with the Rams, a record that stands to this day alongside the record 18 touchdowns he scored that season. The following year he took it to an even higher level, rushing for 2,105 yards, a single-season record that also remains. In fact, Dickerson continues to hold the records for most yards rushing after a player's first, second, third, fourth, fifth, sixth, seventh, and eighth seasons. He remains the only player to rush for 1,800 yards in three different seasons, which he accomplished in his first four years. He reached 10,000 rushing yards faster than any player in history, arriving at the total in just ninety-one games. Further, the 248 yards he rushed for in a playoff game against the Cowboys in 1986 remain the NFL's all-time postseason mark. His coach that day was John Robinson, who remarked afterward, "Eric Dickerson just played as great a game as I've ever seen a man play."

Dickerson was a legend before he made his way to the NFL. He famously ran the 100-yard dash in 9.4 seconds in high school, then teamed with Craig James at SMU to form the vaunted "Pony Express." Chosen second in the 1983 draft behind John

> # ERIC DICKERSON was a legend before he made his way to the NFL.

Elway, NFL teams promptly wore him out. The last of his four rushing titles came in 1988, at which time he claimed four of the top eight seasons in NFL history in total rushing attempts. When he retired after the 1993 season, Dickerson was second only to Walter Payton on the all-time rushing list.

It is difficult to comprehend why Dickerson's place in the pantheon of great backs isn't more secure. Perhaps because he wasn't as flashy as Barry Sanders, as winning as Emmitt Smith, or as versatile as Marcus Allen, it feels as though those contemporaries are often better remembered than he is. Perhaps his highly publicized contract dispute, which led to his departure from Los Angeles for Indianapolis in a ten-player deal, altered the general perception of his career; Dickerson was largely painted as a malcontent, fairly or not so, during that time. Either way, if you ever saw him run, none of the rest of that matters. In the annals of great runners in pro football history there is a large space carved out for Eric Dickerson, and he is well deserving of the number 29 in this compilation as well.

The following is a comprehensive list of all the players in NBA history to win multiple scoring titles, championships, *and* MVP awards:

- Wilt Chamberlain
- Kareem Abdul-Jabbar
- Michael Jordan
- Stephen Curry

It's hard to imagine a more exclusive club a player could join than one made up solely of veritable NBA royalty. The first three are legends that could each stake a legitimate claim to a spot on the all-time Mount Rushmore of the sport. The fourth, the most recent addition, is carving out his own space as we speak, one unlike any the game has ever seen.

(Author's note: This is the final essay I completed for this collection, for the simple reason that Curry was busy chasing a championship while the other ninety-nine were being written.

As I type these words, in June 2022, Curry is less than a week removed from adding the most significant brushstrokes yet to a masterpiece that appears nowhere near finished. By capturing the 2022 title, dominating the playoffs, and being named MVP of the finals, Curry cemented his place among the greatest ever to play the game. All the records listed below are as of the end of the 2021–22 season.)

With Curry, there is one easy place to begin: He is the greatest shooter that ever lived. He has the highest free throw percentage in NBA history at 90.8 percent. He has hit 130 shots of more than thirty feet from the basket, against just 26 dunks. In December 2021, he passed Ray Allen (2,973) for most made

> # There can be no legitimate discussion of the greatest players in basketball history that does not include **STEPH CURRY**'s name.

three-pointers in history—and he's still going. Allen achieved that total in 1,300 games; it took Curry only 789 to break it. Allen made a then-record 269 threes in 2005–06. Steph made 272 in 2012–13 to break it, then 286 in 2014–15 to break it again, and then 402 in 2015–16, which remains the record. In all, Curry has four of the top five individual three-point seasons in NBA history. He has twenty-two career games with at least 10 made threes; no other player has more than five.

All those numbers boggle the mind, and, in my opinion, occasionally work against the perception of his historical greatness. For much of his career, Curry has been talked about like a carnival act. *Come see the little guy who can shoot from anywhere!* The truth is so much greater than that, and perhaps his latest championship will enable perception to catch up with reality. Consider that with his fourth title, Curry joins LeBron James, Tim Duncan, Michael Jordan, Magic Johnson, Kareem Abdul-Jabbar, and Bill Russell as the only players with four rings and multiple MVPs. That's not a novelty act, it's an immortal.

Also worthy of note is the way in which Curry has changed the game. When he entered the league, teams were attempting 18 threes per game on average. By 2021–22, that number had practically doubled. Certainly, number 30 for the Golden State Warriors is not the only cause of this phenomenon, but he has undoubtedly been at the center of the explosion of outside shooting as the first player to prove that championships could be earned so far from the rim.

As I write this, debates are raging over whether Curry is among the ten greatest basketball players that ever lived. The simple fact we are asking the question demonstrates how historic his achievements have been. For me, it goes like this: There can be no legitimate discussion of the greatest players in basketball history that does not include Steph Curry's name. I'm not sure there is any higher praise for an athlete than that.

It is as famous a photo as the world of sports has ever produced, yet its own subject was never even aware of its existence. The only person in the photo is a man named Ron Turcotte, but even he has spent his life acknowledging that he is not what makes the image so special. The subject of the photo is the thoroughbred upon which Turcotte sits, as together they approach the finish line at the 1973 Belmont Stakes. The jockey is peering backward to see for himself what the rest of the world already knew: Secretariat was the most spectacular horse in the history of racing.

When Secretariat crossed that finish line, becoming the first Triple Crown winner in a quarter century, he was thirty-one lengths ahead of the field, which remains the record for any Triple Crown race and ranks among the most dominating performances in the history of any sport. The gap was so wide the CBS cameras could barely show Secretariat in the same

IN A SINGLE YEAR,

SECRETARIAT

ESTABLISHED NEW RECORDS IN EACH OF
THE SPORT'S THREE MOST IMPORTANT RACES,
NOT ONE OF WHICH HAS BEEN BROKEN IN THE
HALF-CENTURY THAT HAS PASSED SINCE.

shot as his competition. Charles Hatton summed it up best in the *Daily Racing Form*: "His only point of reference is himself."

You could make an argument there was never a better year in any sport by any athlete than Secretariat in 1973. First came the Kentucky Derby, often described as the "most exciting two minutes in sports." That year, Secretariat became the first ever to run that race faster than two minutes—his winning time of 1:59.40 remains the record. Next came the Preakness, where Secretariat's winning time of 1:53 remains the event record. And then, finally, the Belmont, and a winning time of 2:24 that has never been approached. In a single year, Secretariat established new records in each of the sport's three most important races, not one of which has been broken in the half-century that has passed since.

In so doing, the horse known as Big Red became a cultural touchstone, gracing the covers of *Time*, *Newsweek*, and *Sports Illustrated* in the same week. Over five thousand winning tickets for that year's Belmont Stakes were never redeemed because they carried greater value as souvenirs. Today there are 263 roads named for Secretariat, more than for any other athlete, human or otherwise.

What made the horse resonate so deeply in that moment in American history? Iconic chronicler George Plimpton offered this explanation: "He was the only honest thing in this country at the time. This huge, magnificent animal who wasn't tied up in scandal, wasn't tied up in money, he just ran because he loved running." Those 31 lengths at the Belmont are a record that figures never to be broken. Human or not, Secretariat absolutely deserves the number he captured.

"For mercurial speed, airy nimbleness, and explosive violence in one package of undistilled evil, there is no other like Mr. Brown." Those words were written by the best sportswriter that ever lived, Pulitzer Prize–winner Red Smith, to describe the best football player that ever lived, Jim Brown. Six foot two, 230 pounds with a thirty-two-inch waist, Brown dominated the sport in ways no one ever had before, nor since, nor ever will again.

It began immediately; Brown was named the MVP of the NFL in his rookie season, 1957, still the only rookie ever to win the award. He remains the only non-quarterback to win it more than once, earning it three times, including in his final season. Brown played just nine years. He led the league in rushing in eight of them; no other back ever did so more than four times. Brown also led in total yards from scrimmage six times, another feat no other back ever did more than four times. He remains the only back to average over one hundred yards rushing per game (104.3) and is the all-time leader in scrimmage yards per game (125.5); with those numbers, Brown would have averaged 1,773 rushing yards and 2,133 scrimmage yards in seventeen-game seasons. Further, Brown is the only player ever with more touchdowns scored (126) than games played (118). Those touchdowns also stood as the career record until Jerry Rice broke it in 1994, requiring twenty-three more games—nearly two full seasons in Brown's era—to make up the ground.

Jim Brown's teams in Cleveland were perennial powerhouses, with number 32 directly at their core. The Browns rode their star back all the way to the 1964 NFL championship, defeating John Unitas and Baltimore in the title game behind 151

> # There have been many great football players, and there will be plenty more, but there will only ever be one **JIM BROWN**.

total yards from Brown—the last championship the Cleveland franchise has won. In all, the Browns played 122 games during Brown's career, including the playoffs, and he played in every one of them.

We will never know the numbers Brown might have achieved

had he not retired prematurely at the age of twenty-nine. While working on the movie *The Dirty Dozen* following the 1965 season, Brown stunned the sports world, announcing he wanted to devote more time to his movie career and to race relations, which he most certainly did. Brown went on to appear in more than thirty films and made an enormous mark with, among others, the Negro Industrial Economic Union, which assisted Black-owned businesses, and the Amer-I-Can program, an effort to turn gang members from destructive to productive members of society.

Jim Brown wore number 44 at Syracuse, where he was also considered among the greatest lacrosse players in the history of that sport, and was named the greatest college football player ever by ESPN on the sport's 150th anniversary in 2019. He was number four on the *SportsCentury* list of the greatest athletes of the twentieth century, the highest ranking for any football player. He was, quite simply, the best ever. There have been many great football players, and there will be plenty more, but there will only ever be one Jim Brown.

33

Ask a bunch of basketball fans who the greate
time was, and most of them will say Michael J
people are wrong. Jordan was probably the *bes*
he would be my choice for that. But *best* is a d
surement; it is subjective, thus it implies that yo
relevant to the answer. To be the *greatest* is some
other than that, something that must be mea
tively, and by that standard the only correct ansv
Abdul-Jabbar, the most accomplished athlete in
American team sports.

Lew Alcindor, as he was then known, is univers
edged to be the greatest high-school player and
lege player ever. Wearing number 33, he led Pov
Academy in New York City to three straight champ
a seventy-one–game winning streak. Next came
he was not eligible to play as a freshman. In his

a sophomore, number 33 served notice with 56 points and 21 rebounds. UCLA went 88–2 during his tenure, winning three straight NCAA titles, and Alcindor remains the only man ever to be named Final Four Most Outstanding Player three times.

Again donning 33 in the NBA, in his second season he won his first MVP award and led the Bucks to the title, something the franchise would not accomplish again for another fifty years. In all, Abdul-Jabbar would be named league MVP a record six times, and finish in the top five of the voting *fifteen* times—to put it another way, he was a top-five player in the NBA in fifteen different seasons. He won six NBA championships—as many as Jordan—and led his team to ten NBA Finals appearances.

KAREEM ABDUL-JABBAR,
the most accomplished
athlete in the history of
American team sports.

He broke the NBA's all-time scoring record in 1984, surpassing Wilt Chamberlain's mark, appropriately enough, with a skyhook, Abdul-Jabbar's signature offensive weapon. He won more games than any other NBA player; including the playoffs, he had seventy more wins than Tim Duncan, number two on that list. He is also first all-time in field goals made, third in rebounds, and third in blocked shots, though there he might actually have been first, given that blocks did not become an official statistic until the fifth season of his career. It is beyond dispute: No basketball player ever accomplished more on the floor than Kareem Abdul-Jabbar.

His name became the source of some controversy when he legally changed it in the fall of 1971. Abdul-Jabbar had been a practicing Muslim since his college days. The name he took means "noble, powerful servant." A half-century after the change, the NBA announced the creation of the annual Kareem Abdul-Jabbar Social Justice Award, which seeks to recognize a current NBA player for pursuing social justice efforts. He is a man whose life, on and off the floor, has elevated his sport, his community, and the entire world. The indelible mark he has left deserves to be remembered as long as the game itself is played.

The 1985 Chicago Bears are among the most remembered, and best loved, sporting teams in American history because of their dominance, though, perhaps in equal measure, because of their seemingly endless array of outlandish characters. The punky quarterback, the heavyweight defensive tackle, and the iron-tough head coach were just a few of the leading roles played in one of the most enduring sports soap operas we have ever seen. But what must be said, and dare never be forgotten, is that the very best of them all was Walter Payton, the comparatively quiet running back from Mississippi nicknamed Sweetness.

In 1985, when Payton was perhaps a step past his absolute prime, he generated over 2,000 yards from scrimmage *and* led the Bears in receptions as they finished second in the league in scoring at more than 28 points per game. Payton was the best player on the best team I ever saw.

In totality, the list of achievements compiled by Walter Payton is mind-blowing. At the time of his retirement, he was the all-time leader in rushing yards and yards from scrimmage, plus he remains the Bears' all-time franchise leader in pass receptions. Payton caught 492 passes in his career, more than Paul Warfield or Lynn Swann, both of whom are in the Hall of Fame as receivers. The era of the three-down back began with Payton; there wasn't anything he couldn't do.

Payton rushed for 1,200 yards in ten different seasons, the most in NFL history. He led the league in attempts in four consecutive seasons, the most of any player in the last seventy years. He produced 2,000 yards from scrimmage four times; no

> **WALTER PAYTON** was the best player on the best team I ever saw.

player ever did it more. In 2000, when the Hall of Fame selection committee named the NFL's all-time team, the running backs were Jim Brown and Walter Payton. If I had a vote today, they would still be the top two in the history of the position.

Payton was an iron man—he simply did not miss games. He played with fractured ribs, turf toe, knee injuries, and a separated shoulder. Most notably, one November day in 1977 he played despite having been sick all week with a fever of 104 degrees. It was not certain until kickoff that he would be able to go. He ran for 275 yards against the Vikings that day, an NFL single-game record that stood for more than twenty years.

Walter Payton's tragic death at the age of forty-five from bile-duct cancer sent shock waves through the football community and well beyond. To this day, it remains impossible to believe a man so strong could be gone so young. The NFL Man of the Year Award, the only award that recognizes a player for his community service activities as well as his excellence on the field, was renamed in his honor shortly after his passing and is considered the most prestigious and meaningful award a football player can receive. A fitting tribute to a legend lost too soon: Walter Jerry Payton, number 34, forever the greatest of all the Bears.

In the entire history of basketball, there has never been anyone better at the pure act of putting the ball in the hoop than Kevin Durant. Having watched the sport my entire life, and studied its fascinating history, I do not require statistical support to feel fully comfortable in that conclusion, though I have plenty of it just in case you do. On the night in 2007 that Durant was drafted second overall behind Greg Oden, my colleague Jay Bilas called him "a scoring savant." That's as good a description as I've heard for the man known as the Slim Reaper, who wore the jersey number 35 in college and his first twelve seasons in the NBA.

Durant spent only one year at the University of Texas, but he certainly made it count, averaging 25.8 points and 11.1 rebounds per game, and becoming the first freshman to win the Wooden Award. From there, he made his mark in the NBA immediately, becoming the youngest scoring champion in league history at the age of twenty-one. Through the 2021–22 season, as this chapter is being written, Durant has won four scoring titles; only Wilt Chamberlain and Michael Jordan won more. Jordan and Durant are also the only players to win at least four scoring titles *and* multiple NBA Finals MVP Awards. Durant was always at his best in the finals, particularly in 2017, when he became the first player since Shaquille O'Neal in 2002 to score 30 points in every game of a finals. In total, as of this writing, Durant has the fourth-highest career scoring average in NBA history. He averaged at least 25 points in thirteen different seasons, more than Jordan, Kobe Bryant, or Karl Malone; only LeBron James has more such seasons all-time.

> In the entire history of basketball, there has never been anyone better at the pure act of putting the ball in the hoop than **KEVIN DURANT**.

For those not as familiar with advanced statistics, true shooting percentage is a measure of efficiency that takes into account twos, threes, and free throws. By that measure, Durant is the most efficient 25 PPG scorer in NBA history. For his career, he shoots a higher percentage from the floor than Larry Bird or Moses Malone, a higher percentage from two than David Robinson or Karl Malone, and better from the free throw line than Dirk Nowitzki or Chris Mullin. He is also the most recent player to average 30 points in a season in which he played all 82 games. That is a statistic I hold near and dear; I genuinely fear he may be the last ever to do it. Durant is also among the greatest international players of all time: a three-time Olympic gold medalist, and the career leader for Team USA in total points, scoring average, made field goals, made free throws, and made three-pointers.

The era in which Durant has played is a complicated one for superstars, and he has often injected himself into the debate over his place in the game's history. That is his choice to make, of course, though I have always viewed that engagement as beneath him. Kevin Durant is the greatest pure scorer that ever lived, and one of the very best players ever as well. Anyone who tries to argue otherwise is, in my view, far more worthy of being ignored than engaged.

n the entire history of sports, I would argue no athlete ever had a greater or more consequential week than Jesse Owens did in early August 1936. Between the third and ninth days of that month, Owens won gold medals in the 100-meter dash, the long jump, the 200-meter dash, and the 4x100-meter relay, becoming the only athlete to take home four golds from those games.

Those medals cemented his place as one of the greatest athletes in the world, but it was what they represented that made Owens one of the most important figures the world of sports has ever produced.

The 1936 Olympics were held in Berlin in Adolf Hitler's prewar Germany. The stands were filled with Nazi supporters. In later years, Owens would recall the moment Hitler himself entered the Olympic stadium: "I remember seeing Hitler coming in with his entourage and the storm troopers standing shoulder to shoulder like an iron fence. Then came the roar of 'Heil, Hitler!' from a hundred thousand throats. And all those arms outstretched. It

JESSE OWENS

WAS MUCH MORE THAN A GREAT AMERICAN
ATHLETE—HIS STORY IS AMONG THE MOST
MEANINGFUL IN THE LONG AND RICH HISTORY OF
SPORTS AND DESERVES TO BE TOLD FOREVER.

was eerie and frightening." One German official belittled the American team, complaining it was filled with "non-humans, like Owens and other Negro athletes." By the end of that August week, Jesse Owens, the son of a sharecropper and grandson of slaves, had singlehandedly crushed the myth of Aryan supremacy.

Jesse Owens had been no stranger to prejudice. Long before he arrived in Nazi Germany, he faced discrimination at home. When he enrolled at Ohio State in 1933, he was barred from living on campus because of his race. Never deterred, Owens dominated track and field, competing in forty-two events his junior year and winning them all. On May 25, 1935, he set five world records and equaled a sixth, all within the span of forty-five minutes. In 1950, the Associated Press named Owens the greatest track and field athlete of the half-century, outpolling Jim Thorpe by a three-to-one margin.

When Owens made his triumphant return from Germany, he was greeted with a ticker-tape parade. But he was not invited to the White House, and he did not receive so much as a message from the president. Owens was stung by the discourtesy. "I wasn't invited to shake hands with Hitler, but I wasn't invited to shake hands with the president, either."

In the end, Owens would win again. In 1976, forty years after Berlin, President Ford presented Jesse Owens with the Medal of Freedom, the highest honor the United States can bestow upon a civilian. In 1984, four years after Owens's death, a street in Berlin was named after him. A few years later, President George H. W. Bush posthumously awarded him the Congressional Gold Medal for his "unrivaled athletic triumph, but more than that, a triumph for all humanity." Jesse Owens was much more than a great American athlete—his story is among the most meaningful in the long and rich history of sports.

As a young boy in Texas, Doak Walker grew up practically in the shadow of Ownby Stadium, the home of SMU football. He attended high school games with his mother in the stadium on Friday nights, and SMU games with his father on Saturdays. When he was old enough, he sold popcorn and peanuts at the games. Years later, when Walker was a student athlete, his fame and notoriety became so great that SMU moved its home games from the stadium he grew up in to an expanded Cotton Bowl, which later honored his legend with a plaque at its main entrance that reads THE COTTON BOWL, THE HOUSE THAT DOAK BUILT.

Walker was a megastar of the college game, winning the Heisman Trophy in 1948, and finishing third on two other occasions; the only player to finish top three in Heisman voting three times since then is Herschel Walker. His Heisman-winning 1948 season was truly one for the ages, in which Walker—a veritable jack-of-all-trades—created 1,119 yards of total offense (rushing, receiving, and passing), plus intercepted five passes, averaged 42 yards per punt, and completed 55.3 percent of his throws (in an era when anything over 50 percent was exceptional). His SMU teams finished in the top ten of the AP poll twice during his career, in 1947 and 1948; the Mustangs would not do so in consecutive years again until the 1980s, the era for which the school ultimately received the NCAA "death penalty." Doak Walker was the MVP of back-to-back Cotton Bowls, leading his teams to a record of 18–1–3 in those two seasons. Today, the Doak Walker Award honors the nation's

> # DOAK WALKER was a superstar long before the term itself was used.

best running back among FBS juniors or seniors who combine outstanding achievements on the field, in the classroom, and in the community.

Walker's accomplishments as a pro, while perhaps not as well remembered, were equally exceptional. Playing for the Lions, he was the NFL's leading scorer in his first (1950) and last (1955) seasons. His total of 128 points as a rookie was second in NFL history at the time. When he retired after just six seasons, he was the fourth-leading scorer in NFL history. His Lions won the championship in 1952 and 1953, beating the Browns in both title games; Walker scored 17 of the Lions' 34 points in those games. Such was Walker's brilliance that he was inducted into the Pro Football Hall of Fame despite playing just those six years.

Doak Walker wore number 37 both in college and the NFL; it was subsequently the first number ever retired by SMU, then the first retired by the Lions. He was a superstar long before the term itself was used. "He was as golden as golden gets," wrote the award-winning columnist Rick Reilly. "He had perfectly even, white teeth and a jaw as square as a deck of cards and a mop of brown hair that made girls bite their necklaces. He was so shifty you couldn't have tackled him in a phone booth, yet so humble that he wrote the Associated Press a thank-you note for naming him an All-American."

Long before Diana Taurasi or Sue Bird. Before Sabrina Ionescu, Breanna Stewart, or Maya Moore. Before Brittney Griner or Geno Auriemma or Lisa Leslie or Rebecca Lobo, there was Pat Summitt. And had it not been for her, there may never have been any of the rest.

There was no NCAA basketball tournament for women when Summitt began coaching at Tennessee. Paid less than nine thousand dollars her first season, she once held a doughnut sale to help pay for the team's uniforms, which she washed herself. Her teams sometimes slept on mats in the opponents' gyms because there was no money for hotels. It is not an overstatement in any way to say that Summitt, the fiery, legendary coach, is the most important person in the history of her sport. Auriemma, who broke most of the records Summitt set, is the first to say so. "She was the one that everyone tried to emulate," said her longtime rival. "That was the program everyone tried to be."

Pat Summitt coached thirty-eight seasons, all of them at Tennessee, and never had a losing record. From the time of the inception of the women's tournament—forty-three years after the men's—Summitt coached thirty-one seasons and made the Big Dance in every one of them. In all, she coached her teams to eighteen Final Fours; at the time of her last appearance, no other coach, men's or women's, had made it to more than twelve. She coached eight national championship teams and twenty-one All-Americans. More importantly, every single

PAT SUMMITT, the fiery, legendary coach, is the most important person in the history of women's basketball.

player who completed her eligibility during Summitt's tenure graduated from the University of Tennessee.

Pat Summitt was named the Naismith Coach of the Century in 2000. She was once approached by Tennessee officials about coaching the men's team and dismissed the overture, asking, "Why is that considered a step up?" Her intensity was the stuff of legend. Her hands pounded the court so hard that she sometimes flattened the rings on her fingers and had to have them re-rounded in the off-season. When she gave birth to her only child, Tyler, in 1990, she went into labor while on a recruiting trip in Pennsylvania and urged the pilots to fly her home so her son would be born in Tennessee.

In August 2011, Summitt revealed that she had been diagnosed with early-onset dementia and was forced to prematurely step away from a program, and a sport, she had built from the ground up. She died in June 2016 at the age of sixty-four. Perhaps the best summation of what Pat Summitt and her thirty-eight years at Tennessee meant to the world came from President Obama, when he awarded Summitt the Presidential Medal of Freedom in 2012. "When I think about my two daughters, who are tall and gifted," he said, "knowing that because of folks like Coach Summitt they're standing up straight and diving after loose balls and feeling confident and strong, then I understand that the impact these people have had extends beyond me."

39

Of all the debates in which people occasionally e
sports, none is dumber or more pointless tha
diminish female athletes by making comparison:
counterparts. The most prominent recent exampl
notion that because the twentieth-ranked male
in the world would defeat Serena Williams, he is
tennis player than she is. Do yourself a favor: If
anyone say that, stop listening to that person—
and forever.

Williams is the greatest tennis player of her ger
s a fact, and it requires no qualifier or equivoca
her domination of the sport she plays places her
ist of greatest athletes in our nation's history. The
of her accomplishments that follows is complete
2022 season, when she announced her evolutic
he sport. I had the privilege of attending her f

SERENA WILLIAMS

IS THE GREATEST TENNIS PLAYER
OF HER GENERATION.

the U.S. Open in September of '22. It was genuinely one of the most thrilling nights I have ever spent in a sporting arena. The admiration and love she spent two decades accumulating was on deafening display. It was a night no one in the building will ever forget.

Meanwhile, the number selected as Williams's here represents her 39 Grand Slam titles, including 23 in singles, which is the most by any woman in the Open Era and is one shy of the all-time record held by Margaret Court. She is the only woman in the last eighty years to win seven singles titles at multiple Grand Slam events. Her 365 career match wins at Grand Slams are easily the most ever; Martina Navratilova is second at 306. Williams spent 186 consecutive weeks ranked number one in the world from February 2013 through September 2016, tied with Steffi Graf for the longest streak of its kind; Williams's match record was 209–19 during that stretch. The two legendary "Serena Slams" spanned four consecutive majors each in 2002–03 and 2014–15, during which Williams went 56–0, losing but fourteen sets. During her prime, the media made great efforts to establish Maria Sharapova as Williams's rival, but, as I often say, what a hammer and a nail have is a relationship, not a rivalry; Williams was 20–2 against Sharapova, seventeen of those wins coming in straight sets.

It was, however, Williams's longevity that set her career apart from those of the other great champions of the sport. She won her first Slam at the age of seventeen and won the Australian Open at the age of thirty-five. She is also the oldest Wimbledon champion, and the oldest French Open champion. She won ten Slams after turning thirty; no other woman in the Open Era has more than three such wins. Further, she reached sixteen

Slam finals after turning thirty; no other woman in the Open Era reached more than ten. In total, she reached at least one Grand Slam final in thirteen consecutive years.

I first met the Williams sisters when they were just beginning their journey to international stardom. I recall being struck at the time by their poise and determination. Little did I know what lay ahead for them both. The extraordinary story of Serena's, and her sister Venus's, rise to fame has been told in books and Oscar-winning motion pictures; it is one of the great triumphs in sports history. As a lifelong fan of the sport, it has been a delight for me to watch every stage of their brilliant careers. And for Serena, in particular, that brilliance was such that there is no way to assemble a collection of the all-time greats without carving out a place for her.

40

The great game of football has been around for [j...]
hundred years, and it is no stretch to argue that, in[...]
Gale Sayers ran with the ball better than any oth[...]
ever played it. He just didn't do it for very long.

For his career, the Bears' number 40, aka the Ka[...]
produced 9,435 all-purpose yards in just sixty-e[...]
That average of nearly 139 yards per game remain[...]
for any player in the history of the sport. He scor[...]
downs as a rookie in 1965, another record that sti[...]
an aside, consider the Bears' 1965 draft, in whic[...]
aged to select Dick Butkus and Sayers with conse[...]
in the first round.) In only his fifth NFL game, S[...]
on a rush, a reception, and a kick return; the nex[...]
that in a game was Tyreek Hill in 2016. Six of the [...]
Sayers scored as a rookie came in his thirteenth g[...]
in December 1965 against the Forty-Nin[...] Say[...]

have had the single greatest game in history that day at muddy Wrigley Field; the average for his 6 touchdowns was 41 yards. It took fifty-five years before any other player scored six times in a game. Years later, Sayers would note that nobody on the Bears' bench knew it was a record when legendary coach George Halas sat him down and sent in substitutes. Had he stayed in the game, Sayers imagined he might have had 8 touchdowns.

Devastating knee injuries in 1968 and 1970 ended Sayers's career far too early, though not before he had made a lasting impact. Sayers still owns the highest kickoff-return average in NFL history at 30.6 yards. He led the league in all-purpose yards three seasons in a row; only Jim Brown owns a longer

> **GALE SAYERS**'s impact on the culture will likely last longer than any of his records.

streak. In 1994, Sayers was named to the NFL's seventy-fifth anniversary team at two different positions, running back and kick returner. He remains the only Pro Football Hall of Famer enshrined before the age of thirty-five.

Gale Sayers's impact on the culture will likely last longer than any of his records, thanks to his friendship with teammate Brian Piccolo. During the 1969 season, Piccolo was diagnosed with embryonal cell carcinoma and died the following spring. Their relationship and love for each other became the made-for-TV movie *Brian's Song*, which won five Emmy awards. All I will say of that film is this: Even all these years later, if you watch it and do not cry, there is something wrong with you. It is one of the most genuinely beautiful and heartrending stories ever made in the sports milieu. Still, it is for his brilliance *on* the field that Sayers earns his place on this list. "People will say there were better players, but I don't know who they are," his Hall of Fame teammate Mike Ditka once said. "I don't know anybody that ran the football any better than Gale Sayers."

New York likes to think of itself as the epicenter of sports, and there has never been a time that was more true than during a seventeen-month stretch from January 1969 through May 1970. It began with the Jets and Joe Namath winning Super Bowl III and was bookended by Willis Reed limping onto the Madison Square Garden floor as the Knicks won the NBA championship. Sandwiched in between those two events was the team known forever as the "Miracle Mets," who, in 1969, became among the most improbable champions in World Series history. Of all the players on all those New York teams, Tom Seaver was historically the greatest. Joe Namath may be the most legendary, and Walt Frazier the most stylish, but Tom Terrific was nothing less than one of the greatest pitchers that ever lived.

The Mets were the worst team in baseball during the five years preceding Seaver's joining the team in 1967. Two years later, he threw a ten-inning complete game in the World Series, and the Mets won the title the following night. Seaver was *Sports Illustrated*'s Sportsman of the Year in 1969, winning his last ten decisions and the Cy Young Award after finishing 25–7. During the first ten seasons of his Mets career, Seaver averaged 18 wins, 16 complete games, and struck out 2,334 batters. On April 22, 1970, Seaver struck out 10 consecutive batters to conclude a game, a record that has still not been surpassed. Every Mets fan above a certain age will vividly recall the night Seaver was dealt to Cincinnati, a deal known as the Midnight Massacre. For a franchise that has had its share of difficult times, that remains its darkest day.

TOM SEAVER was the first player to enter the Hall of Fame wearing a New York Mets cap.

For his career, Seaver won 106 more games than he lost, which is remarkable considering he pitched for only four playoff teams in twenty seasons. He struck out 200 batters in ten different seasons, which remains a National League record. In 1981, he became the fifth pitcher in history to reach 3,000 strikeouts. Four years later, he became the sixth live-ball pitcher to reach 300 wins. Seaver was selected to the Hall of Fame on the first ballot in 1992 with 98.8 percent of the vote, which remains the highest percentage for any starting pitcher ever. He was the first player to enter the hall wearing a New York Mets cap.

Among my favorite stories about Tom Seaver is the day he did not become a Dodger. Seaver was studying dentistry at USC when he was drafted by the Dodgers in 1965. The legendary Tommy Lasorda offered Seaver a signing bonus of two thousand dollars. Seaver responded by asking for fifty thousand. "Good luck in your dental career," Lasorda is said to have replied, and thus was history blissfully rewritten for the fans in New York. If you were to make a list of the greatest legends in that city's illustrious sports history, it wouldn't take you long to get to number 41, Tom Seaver.

"A life," said Jackie Robinson, "is not important except in the impact it has on other lives." In the entire history of sports, it is very likely that no life ever had a greater impact on all of society than did his.

Growing up in the public schools in nearly all-white Pasadena, a young Jackie was told by a guidance counselor that most likely he would become a gardener. Instead, Robinson went on to become the first UCLA athlete ever to letter in four sports, excelling in football, basketball, and baseball, not to mention becoming an NCAA champion long jumper. Decades later, the baseball stadium at UCLA would be named Jackie Robinson Stadium.

April 15, 1947, will forever remain the most important date in the history of American sports. A slew of books and motion pictures and documentaries would be required to adequately tell the tale of that day and its meaning. I'll use this comparatively brief space to make certain that younger sports fans are aware that Robinson was not only the player who broke the color barrier, but he was one of history's greats on the field as well. He changed the sport as a rookie, stealing 29 bases in a season where no one else in his league had more than 14. He was the National League MVP in 1949, leading the league in both hitting (.339) and steals (37)—it would be sixty-six seasons before another player led in both categories. Robinson, in fact, led all of baseball in steals during the span of his career, including

> There will never be another **42** in baseball, just as there shall never be any person in sports who makes the impact **JACKIE ROBINSON** did.

20 steals of home, one of the most legendary of which came in game one of the 1955 World Series against Yogi Berra and the Yankees. Robinson's Dodgers won six pennants during his ten-year career, and captured the title in 1955, a team that remains among the most beloved and romanticized champions in sports history.

After his retirement, this grandson of a slave and son of a sharecropper who was told he should be a gardener, instead became a true leader in the civil rights movement, joining forces with Martin Luther King Jr. in becoming an honorary chairman of the Youth March for Integrated Schools in 1958. Later, Dr. King would say: "Jackie Robinson made my success possible. Without him, I would never have been able to do what I did."

On April 15, 1997, a half-century to the day that Robinson forever changed the culture of America, Major League Baseball permanently retired his uniform number across the entire sport. There will never be another 42 in baseball, just as there shall never be any person in sports who makes the impact Jackie Robinson did. His original Hall of Fame plaque, at his request, made no mention of his breaking the color barrier, but with the support of his family it was recast in 2008 to include the phrase "displayed tremendous courage and poise in 1947 when he integrated the modern major leagues in the face of intense adversity."

It is fitting that the man who would come to be known as the King was a rookie the year his father won the first ever Daytona 500, with racing greatness passed from father to son, and with that race—the greatest in the history of American motorsports—coming to define the son's career. It was Lee Petty who won the inaugural Great American Race in 1959, and that same year it was his son, Richard, who was named NASCAR's rookie of the year, driving the car with the number 43 he would make so iconic that the color would come to be known as "Petty Blue."

Richard Petty won his first Daytona 500 in 1964, and his second two years later, making him the first driver to win the race more than once. In all, Petty would win seven times at Daytona, the last in 1981; at that time, no other driver had won more than two. As of this writing, Petty's seven Daytona wins are three more than any other racer; his 781 laps led are 95 more than any other.

In 1967, Petty enjoyed the greatest season in the history of his sport, winning a record twenty-seven races—including ten consecutively—to enshrine another NASCAR record. That year, Petty won the second of his seven Cup Series titles, a record he now shares with Jeff Gordon and Dale Earnhardt. Petty's 200 career Cup Series wins are nearly double the next closest driver on the all-time list; David Pearson and Jeff Gordon, who rank second and third, combined for 198. For his career, Petty ranks first all-time in races started (1,185), most top-five finishes (555), most top-ten finishes (712), most pole positions earned

RICHARD PETTY's impact on his sport extended well beyond the tracks he drove.

(123), and most laps completed (307,836). His final victory came at the Firecracker 400 on July 4, 1984, with President Ronald Reagan in attendance.

Petty's impact on his sport extended well beyond the tracks he drove. He was the first stock-car racer to earn over a million dollars. His marketing appeal redefined the direction the business of NASCAR would take. "When Richard did the STP sponsorship deal it forever changed the business model in American motorsports," said Jack Roush, founder and owner of

NASCAR powerhouse Roush Fenway Racing. "At a time when a lot of people were panicking about money, not unlike today, he and that company presented a solution that changed the face of racing." Petty's trademark cowboy hat and sunglasses became synonymous with NASCAR right alongside the number that graced the sides of his car—the 43 that belongs to the King of American motorsports for the rest of time.

44

Were one to compile a list of the most iconic moments in American sports history, no matter how short that list might be, it could not be complete without including April 8, 1974, the night Henry Aaron's fly ball cleared the outfield wall in Atlanta, and the most cherished record in sports changed hands.

Seen through the lens of history, when number 44 hit number 715 to take the home run title from Babe Ruth, it is a moment of accomplishment and celebration. But when it actually took place that could not have been further from the truth. In the months leading up to the beginning of that season, being on the doorstep of the record, Aaron lived in constant fear of being assassinated. The *Atlanta Journal* had an obituary prepared, just in case. As he approached the mark, Aaron received over 900,000 pieces of mail, much of it spewing hatred; the only American to receive more mail was the president. On the day the record fell, Aaron's mother, Estella, smothered him with a hug as he reached home plate. Not from delight, she said later, but to shield him from snipers. "The Ruth chase should have been the greatest period of my life," Aaron would later say. "And it was the worst."

While Hank Aaron is remembered most for the home run record, and the dignity with which he broke it and later handed it over to Barry Bonds under questionable circumstances, what is often not given enough attention is just how great Aaron was in every aspect of the game. Aaron never hit more than 47 home runs in any season. Instead he remains the only player to hit at least 20 in twenty different seasons, which he

> # HANK AARON's grace and humanity will forever define his legacy.

did consecutively from 1955–1974. Meanwhile, Aaron never struck out 100 times in any season, nor did he ever rank in the top ten most strikeouts in any season of his career.

Aaron is third on the all-time hits list, behind only Pete Rose and Ty Cobb. He amassed nearly 6,900 total bases in his career, over 700 more than second-place Stan Musial. Aaron remains the all-time MLB leader in total bases, RBIs, and extra-base hits. He was the first player ever to reach both 500 home runs and 3,000 base hits. For his efforts, Aaron was selected as an all-star in twenty-one different seasons. His twenty-one consecutive seasons as an all-star are the most in the history of MLB, the NFL, the NBA, or the NHL.

In 1999, MLB created the Hank Aaron Award, given annually to the best hitter in each of the American and National Leagues, an appropriate tribute to as great a hitter as ever lived. But it will forever be Aaron's grace and humanity that define his legacy. Muhammad Ali once called Aaron "the only man I idolize more than myself." Perhaps the best summation of the legendary journey of Hank Aaron came from the man himself. "The way to fame is like the way to heaven," he said. "Through much tribulation."

45

Archie Griffin was born to be a Buckeye. Quite literally, as a matter of fact: He was born in the hospital on Ohio State's campus. If that didn't seem proof enough, in just his second game as a freshman Griffin rushed for a school record 239 yards, and a Buckeyes legend was born. Griffin is the only player to win the Heisman Trophy more than once, but what is subsequently too often overlooked is just how historic the entirety of his college career was.

Griffin was Ohio State's tailback for four seasons from 1972 through 1975. The Buckeyes went 40–5–1 during that time and won the Big Ten all four seasons. As such, Griffin was the first player ever to start in four consecutive Rose Bowls. He had a stretch in which he rushed for at least 100 yards in thirty-one straight regular season games, an FBS record that still stands and seems unlikely ever to be broken. When his career ended, he owned each of the top three individual rushing seasons in Ohio State history. His career rushing total of 5,589 yards remains the school record by more than 1,000 yards. His per-game rushing average of 121.5 yards is more than 15 beyond any other player in the school's history. His Big Ten career record for most all-purpose yards stood for a quarter century before it was broken by Ron Dayne.

In 2013 the Rose Bowl celebrated its centennial, with Archie Griffin named its All-Century Player. Despite the illustrious and star-studded history of the game, it was an obvious choice. Griffin rushed for 412 yards on 79 carries in the bowl they call the Granddaddy of Them All, including 149 yards in his 1974 appearance. Griffin won the Heisman in 1974 and 1975 after

> **ARCHIE GRIFFIN** is best known, of course, for being the only player to win the Heisman Trophy more than once.

finishing fifth as a sophomore in 1973, thus becoming the first player since Doak Walker in the 1940s to finish top five in the voting three times. When college football marked its 150th anniversary, ESPN ranked Griffin as the fourth-greatest player ever. He was elected to the National Football Foundation and College Hall of Fame in 1986, and his number, 45, was retired by Ohio State in 1999. Griffin's collegiate coach, the legendary Woody Hayes, offered the most fitting final words: "He's a better young man than he is a football player," Hayes said. "And he's the best football player I've ever seen."

"My goal," **Babe Didrikson said,** "was to be the greatest athlete who ever lived."

If you want to, you can make a fairly compelling argument she accomplished exactly that.

Born Mildred Ella Didrikson in 1911, she received her nickname in her early teens from the boys who were awed at the long home runs she would hit playing baseball. Late in her life, she played in celebrity golf tournaments with the legend who inspired her nickname, and Didrikson was known to refer to their duo as "The Big Babe and The Little Babe."

The legend of Babe Didrikson began at the 1932 Olympics in Los Angeles. Actually, it began earlier, in July of that year, during Olympic qualifying—a three-hour span in which the twenty-one-year-old won five events and tied for first in another, setting three world records and sharing a fourth in the process. She would ultimately qualify for five Olympic events, though women were allowed to enter only three. So she competed in three, winning two golds and a silver, setting two world records and another Olympic record in the process. She was celebrated with ticker-tape parades in Dallas and her hometown of Beaumont, Texas, though little did her fans know she was only just getting started.

Not long after retiring from track-and-field, Didrikson became the preeminent star of women's golf, beginning as an amateur. By 1935, she was on a tour with that year's Masters champion, Gene Sarazen, winner of seven major championships. Didrikson frequently outdrove him. In 1946, Didrikson had

BABE DIDRIKSON wanted to be the greatest athlete that ever lived. You might argue she did just that.

perhaps the greatest year the sport had ever seen, winning an unimaginable thirteen consecutive events in one stretch; it is that legendary streak for which the number 46 is dedicated to her here. She then won the US Women's Open in 1948, 1950, and 1954, the final victory coming by 12 shots, a record margin that still stands today. In all, Didrikson would win forty-one tournaments as a professional, ten of those coming prior to the LPGA's start in 1950. She still holds the tour record as the player who reached ten, twenty, and thirty wins the fastest.

Didrikson possessed a showmanship and braggadocio that was well ahead of its time, regardless of gender, often arriving at tournaments and announcing to the assembled media: "The Babe is here! Who is going to finish second?"

When Didrikson died of cancer in 1955, at the age of forty-five, President Eisenhower opened a press conference by offering a moving tribute. Didrikson had, by then, been named by the Associated Press as the greatest female athlete of the first half of the century. Decades later, ESPN's *SportsCentury* retrospective recognized her as the tenth-greatest North American athlete of the twentieth century, the highest-ranked female on the list.

"She is beyond all belief until you see her perform," famed sportswriter Grantland Rice once wrote. "Then you finally understand that you are looking at the most flawless section of muscle harmony, of complete mental and physical coordination, the world of sport has ever seen."

47

Do you remember where you were on October 27, 1991?

If you are my age, there's no question you do. You and I were both doing the same thing: watching the Twins beat the Braves 1–0 in game seven of the World Series. It was the single greatest baseball game I ever saw, and it featured the single greatest performance as well, from the winning pitcher, Jack Morris.

Working on three days of rest, Morris threw 126 pitches that night, every last one of which could have cost his team the title. He pitched a ten-inning shutout, allowing no runs on 7 hits and 2 walks, striking out 8. The opposing starter that night was also a Hall of Famer, John Smoltz, and he also allowed zero runs but was pulled with two runners on and one out in the eighth inning. Morris had also found trouble in the top of that eighth, allowing a single and then a double to start the inning, so he faced runners at second and third with nobody out. He got out of the jam, he explained, because he was absolutely certain he would.

"I was in trouble many times," Morris said, "but I didn't realize it because I never had a negative thought." It is stating the obvious, but still worth noting, that in the modern era of baseball no pitcher would be allowed to work through such a jam in a regular-season game, much less the seventh of the fall classic. But Morris's teammate Randy Bush explained to *Sports Illustrated* what he believes would have happened if manager Tom Kelly had tried to make a move. "Jack would have punched him, kicked him . . . He might have killed him."

> Game seven of the 1991 World Series was the single greatest baseball game I ever saw, and it featured the single greatest performance as well, by **JACK MORRIS**.

Morris's legendary performance remains the last shutout in game seven of a World Series. Candidly, the way things are now, it is unlikely there will be another in the foreseeable future. The Morris game is also the only postseason shutout of more than nine innings in over half a century. When Morris was enshrined in the Hall of Fame, the last line of his plaque was written as follows: *Earned 1991 World Series M.V.P. honors, carrying Minnesota to title with 10-inning shutout in Game 7.* Consider, if you will, that choice of words. The performance was so epic they opted to editorialize on his Hall of Fame plaque, something that is very seldom done.

That game is the reason Morris is in the Hall of Fame; while he had a fine career, there is no way he'd be in Cooperstown without it. He led the majors with 162 wins in the 1980s, and his 175 career complete games are the most by any pitcher since 1975. But his career ERA of 3.90 is the highest for any pitcher in the Hall—he never finished in the top four in his league in ERA, he never finished in the top two of Cy Young voting, and his overall postseason career ERA was 3.80.

Still, the purpose of the Hall of Fame is to tell the story of the game, and there is no way that tale can be told without that magical night in 1991, when the pitcher wearing number 47 for the Twins threw perhaps the greatest game in the history of the sport. That night rendered Jack Morris worthy of baseball's most sacred honor, and it earned him a memorable space on this list as well.

48

Rick Hendrick, the enormously successful founder and owner of Hendrick Motorsports, has been involved in auto racing for more than half a century. So when he offers the following opinion on champion driver Jimmie Johnson, the words carry a great deal of weight: "If you just said, 'I'm going to make a list of what the perfect driver would be, from the talent to the ability to work with sponsors, the athlete—he's just raised the bar. . . . From fitness to charity, it's unbelievable how perfect he is."

Jimmie Johnson is, inarguably, the greatest driver of the twenty-first century, and in his prime was about as dominant in his sport as any athlete has ever been. His seven career NASCAR Cup Series championships are tied for the most all-time and include an unprecedented stretch of five in a row from 2006–10. (The previous mark for consecutive titles had been three, set by Cale Yarborough some three decades earlier.) During his five-year reign, Johnson completely owned

JIMMIE JOHNSON

IS, INARGUABLY, THE GREATEST DRIVER
OF THE TWENTY-FIRST CENTURY.

the circuit, winning thirty-five races, more than doubling his closest competitor, Kyle Busch, who won seventeen. Johnson was named the male Athlete of the Year by the Associated Press in 2009, the only driver ever to be so honored. That year, he won seven races, and led for 2,238 laps—858 more than any other driver. His teammate, Mark Martin, summed it up best when the season concluded: "I'm pretty sure that dude's Superman."

In total, Johnson would win eighty-three races between 2002 and 2017, *forty* more than Kyle Busch, who was next on the list during that stretch. Johnson took the checkered flag in twelve of the sport's "crown jewel" races, including the Daytona 500 twice. He also won twenty-nine playoff races from 2004–16; the next-closest drivers were Kevin Harvick and Tony Stewart with eleven apiece.

Johnson drove his entire career for the Hendrick Motorsports No. 48 Chevrolet operation, his home since his premier series debut in 2001. He was labeled as bland, even boring, early in his career, but he ultimately proved to be quite the opposite, evolving into a leading pitchman and one of the most popular drivers on the circuit. The crowning validation of Johnson's impact came from *Forbes*, which named him the Most Influential American Athlete two years in a row. Along with Jeff Gordon, he helped embed NASCAR more deeply into mainstream culture than it had even been before. Still, it is purely for his greatness on the track that Johnson lands on this list. His era is generally considered by most experts to have been the most competitive in NASCAR history, and still he managed to win his seven Cup Championships in an eleven-year period. Thus, the number 48, which spent a generation whizzing across our television screens in a blur of blue, belongs exclusively to Jimmie Johnson forever.

49

The year was 1943, and a young man from [...] Massachusetts, was drafted into the United Sta[...] an effort to avoid kitchen duty, and other undesir[...] [t]ried boxing. The young man had no experience a[...] [q]uickly showed some natural ability, and after h[...] he began to fight as an amateur. That young mar[...] Rocky Marciano.

"He was the toughest, strongest, most complete[...] [f]ighter who ever wore gloves," wrote the famed [co]lumnist Red Smith. "Fear wasn't in his vocabula[...] [h]ad no meaning." All of those traits were neces[...] [in] part because of Marciano's not-so-large size. S[...] [f]oot ten, weighing between 183 and 189 pound[...] [w]as thought to be too short and too light, and [...] [b]ut sixty-eight inches was the shortest of any [...] [c]hamp. Marciano made up for his lack of siz[...]

power. As sportswriter John Schulian said: "When you got hit, you stayed hit."

Utilizing the thundering right hand he nicknamed Suzie Q, Marciano knocked out the first sixteen opponents he faced as a professional, nine of them in the first round. For his career, Marciano knocked out 88 percent of his opponents, the highest percentage of any lineal heavyweight champion dating back to the 1880s. Marciano became the champion in 1952, beating Jersey Joe Walcott, and would never relinquish the title in the ring, remaining the lineal champ from 1952 through 1956, finishing his career 7–0 in title fights. Only one

> # ROCKY MARCIANO
> remains the only World Heavyweight Champion with a perfect record.

of them, the first of his two meetings with Ezzard Charles, went the distance. Marciano was the smaller fighter in all seven of those title bouts.

One of Marciano's most famous fights came in 1951, before he became the champion. On October 26, Marciano knocked out the legendary former champ Joe Louis in the eighth round. The aging Louis had been Marciano's childhood idol, and Marciano famously cried in Louis's dressing room after the fight. Marciano was named *The Ring* Fighter of the Year in

1952, 1954, and 1955. In September of '55, Marciano knocked out Archie Moore at Yankee Stadium. No one knew it was the last time he would grace the squared circle. Seven months later, Marciano announced his retirement from the ring, becoming the first fighter to retire as heavyweight champion since Gene Tunney in 1928. There would not be another until Lennox Lewis, nearly fifty years later.

In 1999, the Associated Press named Marciano the third-greatest heavyweight of the century, behind Muhammad Ali and Joe Louis. But history will remember Marciano for what he had that neither of those great champions did: a perfect record. Marciano remains the only World Heavyweight Champion with a perfect record (49–0), having won every professional boxing fight in his career. That number will forever define Rocky Marciano. As far as I'm concerned, 49 belongs to him.

There is nothing in sports more compelling than a dynastic champion, nothing that brings more attention and interest to a game, nothing that creates more compelling storylines. In the nearly three decades that I have worked at ESPN, there is no question which athletic program has been the most dominant, nor is there any question when it began. The program is UConn Women's Basketball, and it began the moment Rebecca Lobo chose to play there.

Geno Auriemma, the hall of fame coach who recruited Lobo, is well aware of what her decision meant. "Nationally, everybody was aware of who Rebecca was, and to be able to get someone like that to come to the University of Connecticut automatically put us in a different light." Lobo was truly a superstar prospect when she graduated from high school as the all-time leading scorer in the history of the state of Massachusetts, boys or girls. She was also the salutatorian of her graduating class.

THANKS TO
REBECCA LOBO,
MILLIONS OF YOUNG GIRLS
CAME TO LOVE BASKETBALL.

In 1995, she led UConn to its first ever national championship, launching what would become a basketball dynasty. She was named Final Four Most Outstanding Player, AP National Player of the Year, and Naismith Player of the Year. To this day, Lobo holds the program record for career double-doubles with 59. That team went 35–0, only the second undefeated champion in women's D-I history. It would be the first of eleven championships they would win over a twenty-two-year span.

The following summer, Lobo was the youngest woman on the US Olympic team, winning gold on one of the greatest teams ever assembled. The American women won all eight of their games in that tournament by an average of 29 points. Lobo was the first player in UConn history to win a gold medal. Immediately following the games, Lobo became one of three founding players of the WNBA, helping to inaugurate the first professional league for women's basketball. Lobo was inducted into the Women's Basketball Hall of Fame in 2010, and the Naismith Memorial Basketball Hall of Fame in 2017. Her number 50 was retired by UConn in 2019.

It has been my privilege to know Rebecca Lobo over many years as a colleague at ESPN, but of all the stories I have heard her tell, my favorite came from her Hall of Fame acceptance speech. One night, she said, she and her husband were at home watching the UConn men play, when their daughter, four years old, came into the living room. The young girl looked at the television with a puzzled expression and said, "I didn't know boys played basketball."

Thanks in no small part to her mother, there are now millions of young girls who have the opportunity to think that way.

In the early 1970s, the Green Bay Packers had a running back named MacArthur Lane, who gave perhaps the greatest explanation of what it was like to play against legendary Chicago linebacker Dick Butkus: "If I had a choice, I'd sooner go one-on-one with a grizzly bear. I pray that I can get up after every time Butkus hits me."

Football is frequently described as a gladiator sport, one in which the physical brutality is part of the appeal for both the players and the spectators. More than perhaps any other team sport, the primary objective is to intimidate and impose your will upon your opponent. In the entire history of the sport, no player ever did that quite like the Chicago Bears' number 51.

"You mention his name," said Hall of Fame tight end Charlie Sanders, "my body starts aching." As noted earlier, Butkus was drafted by the Bears the same year as Gale Sayers, who would later say the hardest hit he ever took in his career came from Butkus . . . in practice. In October 1971, *Playboy Magazine* described Butkus as "the meanest, angriest, toughest, dirtiest son of a bitch in football. An animal, a savage, subhuman." If all of those can be meant as a compliment, that description probably fit.

Butkus was a son of the Windy City, starring at Chicago Vocational Academy before heading downstate to the University of Illinois, where, as a junior in 1963, he made 145 tackles and forced 10 fumbles, leading the Illini to a Big Ten championship and a Rose Bowl victory over Washington. With the Bears,

> When a panel of coaches was asked which player they would start with if they were building a new team from scratch, their response was **DICK BUTKUS**.

Butkus made the Pro Bowl in each of his first eight seasons; the only linebackers to do that since are Lawrence Taylor and Derrick Thomas. Butkus was the first defensive player voted first-team All-NFL five seasons in a row, and amazingly received MVP votes in three straight seasons despite his team failing to have a winning record in any of them. In 1970, a panel of coaches was asked which player they would start with if they were building a new team from scratch. Their response was Dick Butkus.

The honors, and awe, continued long after Butkus's knee injuries forced him into premature retirement. He was elected to the Hall of Fame in 1979, in his first year of eligibility, and at thirty-six was the youngest defensive player to be enshrined. Decades later, in 2000, Butkus was chosen as the middle linebacker for the NFL's Official All-Time Team Roster by members of the Hall of Fame selection committee. To this day, his name remains synonymous with toughness and intimidation and is spoken with reverence by players far too young to have seen him play.

Perhaps only Butkus himself could explain how he came to be the way he was. "From the Romans to the Native Americans to the US Marine Corps, the battle cry remains the primary method of pushing the fear down so far the whimpering can't be heard," he said. "On the football field, there was no one louder than me."

However great you think the 2000 Baltimore Ravens were on defense, I am here to tell you they were even better than that.

That group achieved a level of dominance seldom seen in any sport. They allowed 10 points per game during the regular season, the fewest of any Super Bowl champion. Then, in four postseason games, they *scored* 2 touchdowns and *allowed* 1. In the conference title game (vs. the Raiders) and the Super Bowl (vs. the Giants) combined, the Ravens defense played thirty drives and allowed a first down on just eleven of them. For the season, including the playoffs, the Ravens went 14–0 in games in which their offense scored a touchdown. While I will always be partial to the 1985 Chicago Bears as the most dominating defense of all time, the alternate argument for this unit is an easy one to make. As is the argument for greatest individual player on either of those two great defenses filled with stars. Ray Lewis simply seemed to want it more than anyone else.

"The greatest leader in NFL history" is what team owner Steve Bisciotti called Lewis, who was without debate the greatest player in franchise history. Lewis was the sort of linebacker, not unlike Dick Butkus, who incited equal parts respect and awe. "He could inspire not only a defense but an entire city," said Tennessee running back Eddie George, one of Lewis's fiercest rivals. "He was the best linebacker I've ever played against," said Peyton Manning, "and maybe the best defensive player I ever played against as well."

Lewis was named NFL defensive player of the year for the 2000 season, and then again in 2003; Lawrence Taylor and

RAY LEWIS simply seemed to want it more than anyone else.

Mike Singletary are the only other linebackers to win that award more than once. Lewis was also the MVP of Super Bowl XXXV, the first linebacker to claim that trophy since Chuck Howley in 1970. Prior to Super Bowl 50, the Hall of Fame selection committee named the Super Bowl Fifty Golden Team and chose two inside linebackers, Jack Lambert and Ray Lewis. Further, Lewis remains the only player in NFL history with 40 career sacks and 30 career interceptions. While tackles are an unofficial statistic, he is the all-time leader in recorded history with 2,059. His twelve Pro Bowls equals Junior Seau for most by any linebacker all-time. In 2018, Lewis was elected to the Pro Football Hall of Fame in his first year of eligibility.

The visions of Ray Lewis emerging from the pregame tunnel, doing his signature "squirrel" dance, inspiring teammates with fiery words as tears ran down his cheeks, are the sort of images fans of any team will never forget, among the most iconic visuals of the era. They serve to tell the story of the legendary linebacker who was neither the fastest, the biggest, nor the strongest, but simply seemed to want it more than anyone else.

"Wins and losses come a dime a dozen," Lewis once said. "But effort? Nobody can judge that. Because effort is between you and you."

There is no image more quintessentially American than that of a cowboy riding in on a horse to clean up whatever mess the town has gotten into. In my lifetime, the embodiment of that image in film has been Clint Eastwood. In sports, it was Nolan Ryan.

Ryan was by no means the best pitcher of all time, nor even of his own time, but he was the most exciting, the most feared. It almost felt like every time he stepped onto the mound, he may as well have uttered, "There's a new sheriff in town" before hurling that lethal fastball past hitter after helpless hitter. The intimidation he brought to the mound began early in his life. The legend goes that, while pitching in high school, Ryan once cracked the first batter's helmet, then broke the second batter's arm, after which the third refused to get in the box. It remained that way when Ryan came up as a Met in 1966, and every day from then until he threw his final pitch as a Ranger twenty-seven years later.

Ryan's dominance and longevity enabled him to achieve any number of milestones that seemed unfathomable before he came along. He threw seven no-hitters, the first and last of which came eighteen years apart. The previous record had belonged to Sandy Koufax, who threw four. Ryan finished his career with 5,714 strikeouts, one of those records that will almost certainly never be broken; Randy Johnson is second all-time, with 839 fewer. Consider: If a pitcher began his career today with 300 strikeouts in his rookie season, and then matched that for the next eighteen seasons in a row, he would still be

NOLAN RYAN really was the sheriff of baseball.

14 shy of Ryan's record. Ryan struck out 383 batters in 1973, which remains the modern-era record. He also struck out eight father-son pairings during his career, which is one of my personal favorite records in baseball history.

Ryan holds various other distinctions of note, including having been America's first million-dollar athlete. He was voted into the Hall of Fame on the first ballot in 1999. But there may be no moment for which he is better remembered than the day Robin Ventura made the unfortunate decision to charge the mound against him. Ryan, famously, wrapped Ventura up like it was a rodeo and delivered what can only be described as *noogies* to the top of the helpless batter's head. "Getting a ballplayer into a headlock," he would later say, "is a lot easier than getting one of those big ol' steers into a headlock." It was the perfect distillation of Ryan's place in the game—he really was the sheriff of baseball. In all, Ryan had his number retired by three different teams, the only pitcher so honored, but we chose his number here for the 53 MLB records he broke or tied during his career. Nolan Ryan was, and remains, a living legend, and absolutely worthy of a place on any list of sports immortals.

If you would like to make some easy money, walk into any sports bar of your choosing tonight and throw out the following trivia question: *Which pitcher who threw at least 500 innings for the New York Yankees has the lowest career ERA?* Then, sit back and collect money from everyone in the room as they all confidently say, "Mariano Rivera." They will all be wrong, and you will be rich. Rivera has the second lowest; the correct answer is Richard "Goose" Gossage, with an ERA of 2.14.

Goose Gossage was "the type of relief pitcher that has become extinct," wrote Murray Chass, the Hall of Fame baseball columnist. That is the perfect choice of word: Gossage had a role that no longer exists, and did it as well as anyone who ever lived. Consider: For his career Gossage recorded more six-out saves (131) than three-out saves (118). By contrast, Mariano Rivera had 25 career multi-inning saves. Gossage had three seasons in which he recorded 10 wins and 25 saves, the most all-time. In 1988, he became only the second pitcher ever with 300 career saves. Twenty years later, he was the fifth reliever ever elected to the Hall of Fame.

For fans of the Yankees who are old enough to remember, 1978 will always be their favorite year. The images and memories are plentiful: the late-season comeback, the one-game playoff at Fenway Park, the brilliance of Ron Guidry on the mound, Graig Nettles at third, Bucky Dent's home run in Boston. What should not be forgotten, though, is that for all the legendary players on that team, the most valuable might very well have

> There is a special place in the history of baseball for the "firemen" like **GOOSE GOSSAGE**.

been Gossage. That season he finished fifty-five games for the Yankees, and saved twenty-seven of them; both of those led the American League. He recorded the final eight outs of the Bucky Dent game in Boston, retiring Carl Yastrzemski for the last out with the tying run at third. Dent was later named the MVP of the World Series with 10 hits, 7 RBIs, and 3 runs scored in six thrilling games against the Dodgers, but all these years later I will still argue Gossage deserved consideration. He finished games two, four, and six, recording six outs in each, allowing no runs in any. He retired the side in the ninth inning of game six to win the series, one of seven times in his career he recorded the final out to clinch a division, league, or World Series title.

It is not the fault of modern-day relievers that they are utilized so differently and asked to do so much less than the closers of previous generations. Rivera is the greatest relief pitcher that ever lived, regardless of anything written above. But there is a special place in the history of the game for the "firemen" like Gossage, and a place for him here as well. Jersey number 54 forever belongs to the Goose.

Quarterbacks in pro football are judged differently from any other players in the sport—or practically any sport, for that matter. Their ability to impact the outcome of games is so disproportionately greater than that of even the best linebacker or wide receiver that only NBA stars are held to a similar standard. Which is to say that for quarterbacks it is not enough to have merely been great; you must have been at your best in the biggest games. Counting rings is both a privilege and a burden, and it is reserved for only the most precious few.

It is by that standard alone that I am willing to acknowledge that Peyton Manning may not be the quarterback with the most complete championship pedigree of all time. His accomplishments in the biggest moments were surpassed by Tom Brady and Joe Montana, among others. However, I hold that over the total course of his career he was the best that ever lived. The consistency of his performance has never been matched, to say nothing of the ways in which he changed the game with the rigor and intensity of his preparation. It is a terrible shame that when the conversation turns to his historical standing there is usually so much said about the minuscule ways in which he fell short.

I chose the number 55 for Manning in honor of the number of touchdowns he threw in 2013, the greatest single season any passer has ever had. The 55 touchdown passes remain the all-time record, 16 more than anyone else had that year. He also passed for a record 5,477 yards while throwing just 10 interceptions, the fewest ever in a 5,000-yard season. Of his

> Over the total course of his career, **PEYTON MANNING** was the best that ever lived.

sixteen starts that year, Manning threw for at least 300 yards and 4 touchdowns a ridiculous *eight* times; no other quarterback has ever had more than five such games in a season. The Broncos scored 606 points that year, another record that still stands.

Manning won his fifth MVP that year, the most all-time. (Worthy of note is that he also finished second in the voting three times, meaning there were eight seasons in his career in which he was among the top two most valuable players in the league.) He was named first-team All-Pro seven times, the most by any quarterback in the Super Bowl era, which is all the more remarkable for having played essentially his entire career concurrently with that of Tom Brady. When Manning retired, he was the NFL's all-time leader in passing yards and touchdowns. He had fourteen seasons with at least 4,000 yards passing; at the time of his last such season, no other quarterback had more than nine. Over the course of his thirteen seasons in Indianapolis, the Colts had the number one offense in the league, scoring 280 more points than any other team in the NFL.

"He is definitely the best quarterback I've coached against," said Bill Belichick, with whom Manning had his most legendary rivalry. The respect Peyton Manning engendered among every constituency in the sport was practically unmatched, and inarguably well deserved. Tom Brady deserves the title of G.O.A.T. for all that he has accomplished, but if you ask me, Peyton Manning was the best I ever saw. No collection of this sort could possibly be complete without him.

The New York Giants had missed the NFL playoffs in seventeen consecutive seasons when in the spring of 1981 a blessed event took place: Lawrence Taylor became available to the franchise with the second pick in the draft. The rest, as they say, is history.

Taylor's thorough domination of NFL offensive lines began immediately, and with his own. Phil Simms, the Giants' quarterback at the time, tells a story of one of the first scrimmages Taylor took part in. The coaches pulled the rookie off the field after just ten minutes, because he had sacked the quarterback on every single throw. Wearing 56, Taylor went on to become the first rookie ever to be named defensive player of the year, an award he would win three times. Along the way, Lawrence Taylor completely redefined the way the position of outside linebacker is played in professional football. It is not a stretch to say that no defensive player in the sport's history ever wreaked more havoc on the opposition.

In 1986, Taylor was named the NFL's MVP, still the most recent defender to be so honored, and only the second ever along with Alan Page in 1971. That year, Taylor beat out Eric Dickerson, who totaled over 2,000 yards from scrimmage, and Dan Marino, who threw 44 touchdowns. The Giants had the number two scoring defense in the league that season and allowed only 23 points in three playoff games en route to the first Super Bowl title in franchise history. Taylor would lead them to another championship four seasons later, helming a team that would rank first in the league in scoring defense. In all, Taylor played in fifteen playoff games and ten playoff wins,

No defensive player in football history ever wreaked more havoc on the opposition than **LAWRENCE TAYLOR**.

both of which remain Giants all-time records. He made the Pro Bowl in each of his first ten seasons, the only post-merger defensive player with that distinction. Bill Belichick was on the Giants coaching staff all ten of those years and has since never wavered in his enthusiastic praise. "I'm not putting anybody in Lawrence Taylor's class," Belichick has said. "Put everybody down below that."

The New York Giants are a legacy franchise, they have been around just about as long as the game itself, and have boasted numerous legendary players, including Frank Gifford, Michael

Strahan, and Eli Manning. But there is absolutely no debate over who is the greatest Giant of them all. The more pertinent historical company Lawrence Taylor keeps are names like Reggie White, Deacon Jones, Joe Greene, Dick Butkus, and Ronnie Lott—the greatest defensive players in history. For my money, Taylor was the greatest of them all. Joe Theismann, who was on the wrong end of the most famous hit of Taylor's career, agrees: "To me, he's the standard by which you measure everything."

People love to call sports records "unbreakable." Particularly in baseball. I have no doubt you have heard that word attached to marks held by Cy Young, Joe DiMaggio, Cal Ripken Jr., and a handful of others. Into that fray I suggest another name, one I don't hear often enough, if ever, in this context. In June 1938, Johnny Vander Meer legendarily pitched back-to-back no-hitters for the Cincinnati Reds, a record that would require someone to (miraculously) throw three in a row to break. It is a safe bet that Vander Meer's name will be in the record book until the end of time.

Interestingly, 1938 was the only season of his career in which Vander Meer wore the jersey number 57. Aside from those two nights his career was respectable but not especially memorable: He was a four-time all-star, including being named the starter in his home ballpark, Crosley Field, the same year as his no-hitters. He led the majors in strikeouts from 1941–43 and was the winningest left-hander in the sport during that span, but for his career Vander Meer finished with more losses (121) than wins (119).

Still, it is what happened on June 11 and 15 of 1938 that made Vander Meer an immortal. The first game was a dominating performance; pitching at home in front of just 5,814 fans, Vander Meer mowed down the Boston Bees, not allowing a single runner to reach second base. Four nights later, Vander Meer found himself in Brooklyn, facing the Dodgers at Ebbets Field. Over 38,000 fans were in attendance this time, as were both Babe Ruth and Jesse Owens, who were part of the festivities

> # JOHNNY VANDER MEER's
> name will be in the record book until the end of time.

surrounding what was the first ever night game on the East Coast. Thus, purely by chance, did two of the greatest sporting legends in American history witness a game unlike any before or since.

The ballpark was filled to overflowing, the Dodgers having sold more tickets than the capacity of Ebbets Field, and so fire department officials had to help clear the aisles and control the overflow crowd. The game was delayed and did not begin until after 9:00 p.m. Vander Meer was forced to warm up three different times. Then he walked the bases full in the ninth inning before getting out of the jam and getting the historic final out when Leo Durocher flew to center. No pitcher had ever thrown multiple no-hitters in a season to that point, much less in consecutive starts. Some tried to suggest that the newness of the lights impacted the Dodgers hitters, which doesn't make sense when you consider the Reds managed six runs on eleven hits. It wasn't until he was in the dugout after the game that Vander Meer learned he had accomplished something no other pitcher ever had. In the eighty-five years that have passed since, none have ever done it again.

The front page of the *Cincinnati Post* on June 16, 1938, proclaimed Vander Meer's double no-hitter the "greatest feat in (the) game's history." A local columnist took the praise one step further even than that, suggesting that a statue to Vander Meer replace one to former President James Garfield in a downtown park, writing, "And then a thousand years from now the citizens will know that John pitched two no-hitters, and pitched them in a row."

58 & 59

Every dynasty in American sports history can be defined by a single image, from Babe Ruth's distinctive waddle around the basepaths to Bill Belichick's hoodie. In my lifetime, the first dynasty I ever saw was the Pittsburgh Steelers of the 1970s, whose everlasting image for me is the snarling, toothless grimace of Jack Lambert, the most menacing member of the iconic Steel Curtain defense. Joe Greene was indisputably the greatest player on those teams, and will receive his just due later in this collection, but that defense, featuring the legendary linebackers Jack Lambert and Jack Ham, deserves a place of its own.

Lambert set a modern-era record that still stands with eight fumble recoveries in 1976, when he was named the Defensive Player of the Year and finished runner-up for MVP. That is the second-highest MVP finish ever for a linebacker, behind

THE STEELERS

HAVE THE ONLY TRUE NFL DYNASTY
TO BE DEFINED BY DEFENSE.

was the ultimate homegrown talent: Raised in Johnstown, Pennsylvania, he played at Penn State before spending his entire twelve-year career with the Steelers. During those years he had 32 career interceptions and 21 fumble recoveries; those 53 takeaways are the most by a linebacker in NFL history. Both "Jacks" were inducted into the Pro Football Hall of Fame in their first years of eligibility. When the NFL announced a Super Bowl 50 Golden Team, the Jacks were two of the four linebackers named, along with Lawrence Taylor and Ray Lewis. Both played their entire careers side by side for the Steelers, Lambert wearing the number 58, and Ham 59.

That era of Steelers football is the only true NFL dynasty to be defined by defense. Despite featuring five Hall of Famers on offense (Terry Bradshaw, Franco Harris, Lynn Swann, John Stallworth, and Mike Webster), there is no doubt those four hard-earned championships were won on the other side of the ball. Consider: The Steelers played eighteen playoff games from 1972 to 1979 and did not allow a 100-yard rusher or 300-yard passer in any of them. During those eight seasons, that defense allowed 190 touchdowns and forced 415 turnovers. In one stretch during the 1976 season, they pitched five shutouts in an eight-game span; no other team in the last seventy-five years has shut out five opponents in any full season.

The Steelers of the seventies remain the only team to win four Super Bowls in a six-season span. They allowed 18 points per game in those wins, giving up a total of 7 offensive touchdowns. Further, in my view they were heavily responsible for the explosion of pro football's popularity in this country. It is no coincidence that it was during this exact era that football replaced baseball as America's most popular sport. The combination of the glamor of the Dallas Cowboys and the blue-collar ruggedness of the Steelers was irresistible. Even those, like me, who were not particular fans of either team, could not help but be taken by their charisma. They were, and for me will always remain, larger than life. We chose the "Jacks" to represent the group, but that entire defense deserves a place on this list; the numbers belong to them all.

I am going to make a statement right now with which you
may disagree. That is your prerogative, of course. But be fully
aware that in this dispute I am 100 percent right and you are
absolutely wrong. The statement is this: The greatest rivalry in
the history of American sports was waged by Chris Evert and
Martina Navratilova, and it isn't especially close.

Larry Bird vs. Magic Johnson, you say? They met in three
NBA Finals, a total of nineteen games played in the championship round. If you choose to include the NCAA championship
game, that makes twenty.

How about Muhammad Ali vs. Joe Frazier? They squared off
in three fights, which lasted a total of forty-one rounds. Two
of the three were for the heavyweight title.

Meanwhile, the immortal sportswriter Bud Collins described
Evert vs. Navratilova as "the rivalry of the century," and he
couldn't have been more right. From 1974 to 1988, the two met

in the final round of *sixty* tournaments. During that time there was a stretch of *twelve straight years* in which one or the other finished ranked as the number one player in the world. In fact, here is how historically great these epic rivals were: They each finished their careers with eighteen Grand Slam singles victories. It is impossible not to assume that either of them would have easily shattered the record of twenty-four had it not been for the other. Further, consider their male contemporaries, Björn Borg and John McEnroe, who met fourteen times in any round of any tournament *total*. Evert and Navratilova met fourteen times in the finals of Grand Slams alone! (Borg vs. McEnroe,

> # The greatest rivalry in the history of American sports was waged by **CHRIS EVERT** and **MARTINA NAVRATILOVA**.

four.) In every one of those fourteen Grand Slam Finals, either Evert or Navratilova was the top seed. As of this writing, those fourteen matches are five more than any other competitors, male or female; Serena and Venus Williams met in nine, the next-most in the women's game. In total, Evert and Navratilova met twenty-two times in Grand Slam tournaments, all of those in the semifinals or finals; no other women in the Open Era have ever met more than eleven times so deep in those events.

Billie Jean King, perhaps the most mythical female athlete

in American history, says of Evert and Navratilova, "They took tennis—not just women's tennis—to a new level." Which they most certainly did, together. As a result, the two women are forever connected, and they both know it. "We brought out the best in each other," Navratilova says. "It's almost not right to say who's better. If you tried to make the perfect rivalry, we were it." Evert is equally aware of their connection. "She was in my life every single day, whether I liked it or not. She was in my life, every single day, for thirty years."

As far as I'm concerned, thirty years was not long enough. Christine Marie Evert and Martina Navratilova deserve to be remembered, together, for as long as the sport is played. In honor of all those finals, and all those memories, the number 60 belongs to them.

In 1927, after Babe Ruth set the home run record with 60, he was not understated in his assessment of his own accomplishment. "Sixty! Count 'em, sixty," the Bambino said. "Let's see some other son of a bitch match that!"

It took a long time. The most hallowed and beloved record in American sports stood for more than thirty years, until 1961, when Roger Maris of the Yankees concluded what became one of the most controversial seasons the sport had ever had. Many forget that Maris was actually the reigning American League MVP that year. It was a season in which two teams were added to the American League, diluting the talent among pitchers, along with expanding the schedule from 154 to 162 games. As the season wore on and Maris closed in on the record, great swaths of the media, many fans, and even the leadership of the sport were openly rooting against him. He received so many death threats an NYPD detective was assigned to protect him; Maris's hair fell out in clumps from the stress. In July, Commissioner Ford Frick announced that the record books should recognize two marks, one for the 154-game season, another for the longer schedule. Frick, it should be noted, began his career as a sportswriter, and was the ghost writer of *Babe Ruth's Own Book of Baseball*.

Maris's teammate, Mickey Mantle, was in every way the golden boy of the age and seemed the one most likely to break the record. In the end, he hit 54 home runs that season; Maris and Mantle remain the only teammates ever to each hit 50 in the same year. Maris, meanwhile, hit his 60th in the Yankees

> Tragically, **ROGER MARIS** did not get to revel in his own achievement.

159th game and number 61 in game 163. As a result, the afore-mentioned commissioner determined there should be an asterisk beside the number in the record book, a designation that remained until six years after Maris died of cancer. In the end, Maris won his second consecutive MVP that year, and the Yankees won the championship, though Maris struggled, batting just .105 in the World Series, perhaps worn-out from the strain of the season.

For 61 years, Maris maintained the American League record for home runs in a season. It can reasonably be stated that he was the only player in that time to hit as many as 61 home runs without being implicated in a steroid controversy, and that he remains one of only two such players in the 150-year history of the sport. Still, he was on the Hall of Fame ballot for fifteen years and did not come close to making it, never receiving more than 43.1 percent of the vote.

Even more sadly, Maris did not get to revel in his own achievement. "It would have been a helluva lot more fun if I had never hit those 61 home runs. All it brought me was headaches," he would say, late in life. "Now they talk on the radio about the record set by [Babe] Ruth, and [Joe] DiMaggio and Henry Aaron. But they rarely mention mine. Do you know what I have to show for the 61 home runs? Nothing, exactly nothing." That strikes me as unjust, if not tragic. For whatever it is worth, the number 61 belongs to him here, and there is absolutely no sign of an asterisk to be found anywhere near it.

It is not a metric that can be measured in any reasonable way, but I do believe it is safe to assume that no person alive ever brought more people to the game of golf—inspiring them to play, or watch, or both—than Tiger Woods. But, if anyone did as much to popularize the sport as Tiger, that person was Arnold Palmer, the leader of "Arnie's Army," and perhaps the most magnetic star in the history of the sport.

"Oh, everything," Tiger has said, when asked what Palmer meant to the growth of golf. "I mean, without his charisma, without his personality in conjunction with TV, it was just the perfect symbiotic growth. You finally have someone who has this charisma and they're capturing it on TV for the very first time. Everyone got hooked to the game of golf via TV because of Arnold."

Palmer's celebrity was so extraordinary that what is often overlooked is just how genuinely great a player he was. Palmer

ARNOLD PALMER'S CELEBRITY WAS
SO EXTRAORDINARY THAT JUST HOW GREAT
A PLAYER HE WAS IS OFTEN OVERLOOKED.

won 62 events on tour; only four players have ever won more. He had a span of seventeen consecutive years in which he won at least once, a record he shares today with Jack Nicklaus. Palmer led the tour in wins in five separate years and won twenty-nine times in a four-year stretch during his prime (1960–63)—still the most wins by a golfer in any four-year period since 1950. Of course, golfers are measured first and foremost by their performance at major championships, and in those Palmer's record stands alongside practically anyone's ever. He won seven majors in all, while only two players in history (Nicklaus and Woods) finished in the top two at more majors than Palmer, who did so seventeen times. Palmer won the Masters four times in seven years; only Nicklaus and Woods won it more, but no one ever won four in a span that short. Palmer was named Athlete of the Decade for the 1960s by the Associated Press and was inducted into the World Golf Hall of Fame as part of its inaugural class in 1974.

Still, while the credentials on the golf course are very much intact, it was the star power he brought to the game that stands as Palmer's most memorable contribution. Gary Player said Palmer fell out of bed with charisma, and the man they called the King maximized the value of that charm in a way almost no athlete in any sport had done before. Consider: Palmer earned $1.8 million during his career on tour; he made *twenty-two times that* in 2015, the year before his death. According to *Forbes*, the only retired athletes to make more money than Palmer that year were Michael Jordan and David Beckham. It is worth noting that Jordan was a year old when Palmer won his last major, with Beckham born eleven years after.

Finally, it is impossible to write about Arnold Palmer without some mention of the drink that bears his name, the delicious combination of iced tea and lemonade that has grown popular well beyond the confines of golf clubhouses. That is perhaps the most obvious way in which Palmer continues to transcend the game he played. But it was his greatness on the golf course that made it possible. In honor of all those times he raised a trophy at the end of a PGA Tour event, the number 62 belongs to Arnold Palmer.

63

...lain once scored 100 points in ar...

...ad a game in which he poured ir...

...plus 15 rebounds, with his team...

...onference finals. But, if you ask m...

...mance by any individual player in a...

...l 20, 1986. The setting was the ic...

...age was the first round of the play...

...chael Jordan.

...of that season are on the short lis...

...istory of the sport. They won 67 g...

..., including a 40–1 record at home...

...entual Hall of Famers and boasted...

...n the sport. Enter the twenty-thre...

...aring number 23 on his jersey. In g...

...dan scored 49 points. Then came gar...

...he postseason record with 63, the...

any player ever scored in any game in the Boston Garden. Among the astonishing subplots of that performance is that it came in a season Jordan missed most of due to a broken foot. The 63-point game was only the twentieth game he played the entire season. The game went to double overtime, with Jordan playing fifty-three of the fifty-eight minutes. "That game represented so much of what is great in sport and basketball," said Bill Walton, one of the Celtics' Hall of Famers.

The 112 points Jordan scored in those two games against that team in that building remain the most by any player in consecutive playoff games. (The next-most was 105, also by

---

MICHAEL JORDAN's 63 POINTS against Boston was the greatest performance by any individual player in an NBA game.

Jordan, in 1988.) They also served notice that the young man from North Carolina was unlike anything the sport had ever seen before. "I always thought that was his coming-out party," said Jerry Sichting, a Boston reserve who made the shot that won that game for the Celtics.

I think so, too. I was a freshman in college when it happened, watching on a small television in my dorm room. That's how special the day was, the kind of performance where decades later you still remember where you were watching it. So, while

Jordan is, of course, already celebrated in this collection, his brilliance in that game is well worth being remembered on its own. If you don't believe me, ask Larry Bird, himself an immortal of the sport, who scored 36 for Boston that day. "He is the most exciting, awesome player in the game today," Bird said after the game. "I think it's just God disguised as Michael Jordan."

Golf is my favorite sport. It has been now for some time, and the space between it and whatever my second favorite is continues to grow. And of all the players in the history of the game, the one who fascinates me most is Ben Hogan.

There are two distinct reasons for this, the first being his swing. If you've never seen it, put this book down right now, go to YouTube, and then tell me it doesn't bring tears to your eyes to see a person do anything as beautifully as that man swung a golf club. "Hogan was the best I've seen," said Jack Nicklaus, the greatest player that ever lived. In fact, when asked if Tiger Woods was the best ball striker he had ever seen, Nicklaus insisted, "No, no—Hogan, easily."

The second fascination I have with Hogan stems from his fierceness; he is universally thought to have been the most intense competitor ever to walk a fairway. "Those steel-gray eyes of his," a friend once said. "He looks at you like a landlord asking for next month's rent." No doubt it was that intensity and focus that enabled Hogan to reclaim his standing as the world's best player after suffering injuries that could easily have killed him. On February 2, 1949, a car Hogan was driving in his native Texas slammed head-on into a Greyhound bus. The impact drove the engine into the driver's seat. Hogan suffered a broken collarbone, a cracked rib, a double fracture of the pelvis, and a broken ankle. It was feared he would never walk again. Sixteen months later, he won the US Open. Hogan won eleven PGA Tour events after the accident, including six of his nine major championships.

> # Of all the players in the history of golf, the one who fascinates me most is **BEN HOGAN**.

If there is a Mount Rushmore of golf, I would argue Hogan belongs on it. Consider, he won fifty-two PGA Tour events in the 1940s, the second-winningest decade in golf history, only four behind the record fifty-six won by Woods in the 2000s. Then remember that Hogan went more than three full years between wins in that decade because of his time serving as a lieutenant in the Army Air Corps during World War II. His consistency of performance was almost unfathomable: In 292 career tournaments, Hogan finished in the top ten 241 times. In 1953, he became the first player ever to win three majors in a calendar year; to this day, Tiger Woods is the only other player to accomplish that. (Notably, Hogan did not play the fourth major, the PGA, that year because of overlapping scheduling.) His season is thus referred to as the Triple Crown: he won the US Open by six shots, the Masters by five, and the Open Championship by four. He competed in five official tour events that year—and won them all.

In all, Hogan would win 64 times on tour, fourth-most all-time, thus the number assigned to him here. But, again, it is Hogan's legendary intensity that fascinates me more than anything. My favorite story is one Hogan himself told about a dream he'd had. In the dream, he played a round of golf and carded seventeen holes-in-one. "I woke up," he said, "mad about the one I missed."

At the funeral for his father in 1987, American track-and-field star Carl Lewis placed an Olympic gold medal in his father's hands. Lewis had won the medal in the 100 meters three years prior. As he left it, forever, Lewis whispered, "I want you to have this because it was your favorite event." His mother was surprised, to say the least.

"Don't worry," Lewis told her, "I'll get another one."

That confidence was well-founded. Over the course of his career, Lewis would compete in ten Olympic events, winning nine and taking silver in the other. The nine golds remain the most for any track athlete since World War II. He won four of those gold medals in the 1984 games in Los Angeles, equaling the accomplishment of his idol, Jesse Owens, in the 1936 Games. Lewis's victory in the 100 meters that year came by an astounding .20 seconds ahead of the second-place finisher, the easiest victory in the race since Bob Hayes twenty years before. Seven years later, at the 1991 World Championships, Lewis would set the world record in the 100 meters; he was, by then, thirty years old.

It was in the long jump, however, that Lewis was truly the best of all time. Over the course of a decade, he won 65 consecutive competitions, hence the number he owns in this list. Lewis still owns five of the top eight longest outdoor long jumps of all time. He also still owns the indoor long jump record (8.79 meters); set in 1984, it is the longest enduring record in a men's field event. He won the long jump in four consecutive Olympics, the last in 1996, when he was thirty-five years old. He and Al Oerter, the discus thrower, are the only track-and-field athletes

CARL LEWIS may well be the greatest track athlete in our nation's history.

to win an event in four straight Olympics. It is worth noting that Lewis may have been even more decorated had it not been for the US boycott of the Moscow Games in 1980; by 1984, he had already ranked number one in the world in both the 100 meters and long jump for three consecutive years.

Simply put, Carl Lewis may well be the greatest track athlete in our nation's history. In 1999, the IAAF, the international track-and-field sanctioning body, honored Lewis as the Male Athlete of the Century. The International Olympic Committee selected him Sportsman of the Century. *Sports Illustrated* named him

Olympian of the Century. So great an athlete was he that in 1984 the Dallas Cowboys drafted him as a wide receiver in the twelfth round, even though he didn't play college football. A month later, the NBA's Chicago Bulls drafted him in the tenth round. That same faith in himself that allowed Lewis to place an Olympic medal in his father's casket ultimately carried him to heights seldom reached in the history of international competition. Which makes his most famous quotation so appropriate to his own story: "If you don't have confidence," he said, "you'll always find a way not to win."

Over the first seventeen years of their existence, the Pittsburgh Penguins won a total of three playoff series. In that seventeenth season, fewer than 7,000 fans regularly attended their home games. Then came season eighteen, when the Penguins selected Mario Lemieux number one in the draft, and nothing was ever the same again.

In Lemieux's first season, attendance increased to over 10,000 per game, a jump of 46 percent. The town was excited about the big, strong, handsome young star from Montreal, and number 66 would spend the rest of his life giving them every reason to be.

The production provided by the man known as "Super Mario" was equaled by one player, and only one, in the history of the game. Together, Wayne Gretzky and Lemieux comprise a remarkable chunk of the game's all-time record book. Lemieux averaged 1.88 points per game for his career, second behind

Gretzky. Lemieux tallied 40 hat tricks in his career; only Gretzky had more. In 1988–89, Lemieux finished with 199 points; Gretzky is the only player ever to reach 200. No other player in history has ever gotten above 155. Amongst the top thirteen scoring seasons in the history of the NHL, nine belong to Gretzky, the other four to Lemieux.

The crowning achievements of Lemieux's career came in the 1991 and 1992 postseasons, in which he led the Penguins to back-to-back Stanley Cups, totaling 78 points in thirty-eight games across both postseasons. He won the Conn Smythe Trophy twice—only Patrick Roy ever won it more. During Lemieux's tenure in Pittsburgh, the Penguins set the NHL records for consecutive regular season wins with seventeen,

> # MARIO LEMIEUX figuratively— and literally—saved the Penguins.

and consecutive playoff wins with fourteen. In all, Lemieux would win three Hart Memorial Trophies as the league MVP; since World War II only Gretzky and Gordie Howe won more. Lemieux also won the Art Ross Trophy as the league's top scorer six times; only Gretzky won more. As of this writing, Lemieux stands eighth on the all-time points list, despite being outside the top 400 in games played.

In addition to nagging back injuries, Lemieux's career was interrupted during his absolute prime by cancer. In January 1993, the Penguins announced the superstar center had been diagnosed with Hodgkin's disease, now known as Hodgkin's lymphoma. Lemieux's battle with the disease, and triumphant return, were inspirational. On March 2, 1993, Lemieux finished his last radiation treatment in Pittsburgh. That night, he had a goal and an assist in Philadelphia. He picked up right where he left off upon his return, earning his fourth scoring title and second MVP, despite missing nearly two months of the season.

In 1999, Lemieux went from being the man who figuratively saved the Penguins to the one who did it literally. The team was mired in financial difficulty, facing bankruptcy. Lemieux was owed millions in deferred salary. He stepped in as the head of an ownership group to buy the team and keep it in Pittsburgh. When the Penguins won their third Stanley Cup Championship in 2009, Lemieux became the only person to ever win the Stanley Cup as both a player and owner.

So, the legend of Mario Lemieux extends well beyond the ice, but let there be no doubt, it was his genius as a player that landed him his place in this compilation. "Mario was one guy that could really motivate me to push my game to another level," the great Gretzky would say. "I knew eventually he was going to chase me down and pull me back. That was inevitable."

When Vin Scully first took his place behind the microphone he would occupy for sixty-seven seasons, the year was 1950. Jackie Robinson batted cleanup that day for the Dodgers, who still represented Brooklyn. The franchise had never won a World Series in its history. The price of a gallon of gasoline was twenty-seven cents. A postage stamp was three cents, the federal minimum wage was seventy-five cents per hour. By the time Scully called his final game as the voice of Dodger baseball, the franchise had relocated to Los Angeles, won six championships, and the cleanup hitter was Yasiel Puig, a man born more than forty years after Scully first took that mic. Thus, when Scully signed off for the final time by saying, "I have said enough for a lifetime," he had literally done just that.

It is impossible to quantify the value of the relationship that can form between a baseball fan and a hometown announcer. The 162 occasions spent together every season can, in some

THERE MAY NEVER HAVE BEEN A PERSON WHO
TOUCHED THE LIVES OF MORE SPORTS FANS IN THE
HISTORY OF THIS COUNTRY THAN

VIN SCULLY.

cases, create connections that feel every bit as real as one has with family and close friends. In my own case, baseball will sound like Phil Rizzuto's voice for as long as I live, and, while I never met him in person, Harry Caray was absolutely the first friend I made when I moved to Chicago for college. Considered in that way, there may never have been a person who touched the lives of more sports fans in the history of this country than Vin Scully. There also may never have been anyone more universally beloved; I have been in the sports media business more than thirty years and, truly, I have never come across anyone who expressed a single foul word about the man.

To simply run down a list of moments and games Scully called hardly does justice to his impact, though the list in and of itself is astounding. Scully called twenty-five World Series and a dozen All-Star Games. He called Kirk Gibson's home run in game one of the 1988 World Series, Hank Aaron's 715th in Atlanta, and Barry Bonds's record-breaking seventy-first in 2001. He called Johnny Podres's shutout of the Yankees in game seven of the 1955 World Series, which clinched the only title the Dodgers ever won in Brooklyn. He called Bill Buckner's error in game six of the 1986 World Series. He was twenty-five years old when he broadcasted his first World Series game, still the youngest announcer ever to do so. He called twenty-one no-hitters, including all four thrown by Sandy Koufax, as well as the only perfect game in postseason history, thrown by Don Larsen. For all of those moments, and for too many more to fathom, Scully was inducted into the National Baseball Hall of Fame in 1982, the same year as Frank Robinson and Henry Aaron.

Somehow, even mentioning that Scully was named the

top sportscaster of all time by the American Sportscasters Association in 2009 feels insufficient to fully explain his impact. Vin Scully was so much more than a great broadcaster. He was a friend, even if you never met him, a trusted and beloved voice on a hot summer afternoon or a crisp autumn night, for as long as practically any sports fan alive can remember. In the entire sporting history of our nation, there aren't but a handful who have left anywhere near the mark he did on our ears, our minds, or our hearts.

Of all the years in the history of Major League Baseball there have been few as memorable, or as consequential, as 1968, known as the Year of the Pitcher. That season changed the game in ways that are still very much felt today, and the pitcher most responsible for that was the Hall of Famer Bob Gibson. A half-century later, his opponents still describe Gibson with a healthy combination of admiration and fear. "The only people I ever felt intimidated by in my whole life were Bob Gibson and my daddy," said Dusty Baker, expressing a sentiment that seemed to hold true for pretty much every hitter in the National League.

In 1968, Gibson went 22–9, allowing 38 earned runs in 304.2 innings. That ERA of 1.12 has never been approached since; the closest was Dwight Gooden at 1.53 in 1985. The 38 earned runs allowed are 19 fewer than any live-ball pitcher has ever had in a 300-inning season. In one stretch from June 6 to July 30,

Gibson allowed three runs across eleven starts (99 innings), all of which were complete games. He finished the regular season with thirteen shutouts, still the most by any pitcher in the live-ball era. He was named National League MVP for the season; Clayton Kershaw was the next pitcher to win the award, forty-six years later.

Gibson also led the Cardinals to the World Series in 1968 and, once there, elevated his performance to levels the game has seen on only the very rarest of occasions. He struck out thirty-five batters in that World Series, which remains the most all-time. Incidentally, the record he broke was his own,

BOB GIBSON was so good in **1968** that baseball had to make changes to give the poor hitters a chance.

set four years earlier. In game one of the series, Gibson struck out seventeen Detroit Tigers, still the most ever in a postseason game. He threw 144 pitches that day. Including the World Series, Gibson recorded 995 outs across thirty-seven starts in 1968, which is 26.9 outs per start. (Here I offer a reminder, should you need one, that a nine-inning game only requires twenty-seven outs.) Gibson exceeded nine innings five times that season, and pitched fewer than eight only twice. His thorough domination of the sport, along with that of several other pitchers, led to the lowering of the mound by five inches in 1969, in an attempt to inject more offense back into the game. Bob Gibson was so good in 1968, baseball was required to make a fundamental change to give the poor hitters a chance.

The rest of Gibson's career was almost equally exceptional. He is one of three players to win multiple World Series MVP awards, Sandy Koufax and Reggie Jackson being the others. Six of Gibson's nine World Series starts came on three days' rest or fewer, and he finished eight of those nine games. In 1974, Gibson became the second pitcher in history with 3,000 strikeouts, Walter Johnson having been the first.

Gibson was actually a great all-around athlete. In fact he held Creighton University's basketball scoring record until Paul Silas broke it. Gibson signed two contracts after college—one with the Cardinals, the other with the Harlem Globetrotters, and for a time he roomed with Meadowlark Lemon. But it was, of course, in baseball that he made his legend. And for all that athleticism, it was his competitiveness that Gibson credited most for his success. "I've played a couple of hundred games of tic-tac-toe with my little daughter and she hasn't beaten me yet," he once said. "I've always had to win."

69

te this, we as fans are living throu
ennis, blessed to be witnessing the
reatest players to ever live: Roger Fe
ovak Djokovic. In tennis, as in ar
t eras tend to be those defined by m
s nothing more exciting than a riva
s why Rod Laver isn't better rememl
stralia—it may have been his mis
ominate his era that no name has e

, as Laver was known, stood only f
only 145 pounds, but as ESPN analyst
physical point of view, he's not ove
nce is enormous." So, too, is his left
toonish in size, enabling Laver to a
strokes, and dominate with his ser

style. Laver's era was the decade of the 1960s. To suggest he "owned" the age might actually be selling his supremacy short. He was only eligible to play in the major tournaments in five of those ten years, due to amateurism policies, but he reached the finals in sixteen of the nineteen in which he played, winning eleven. He won the calendar Grand Slam twice, in 1962 and 1969. He remains the only tennis player, men's or women's, to do so. Among the men, he remains the most recent winner of the Grand Slam, and one of only two ever to accomplish the feat, after Don Budge in 1938. In all, Laver concluded the decade with a match record of 104–8 in Grand Slam events.

ROD LAVER may have had the misfortune to so thoroughly dominate his era that no name has ever belonged alongside his.

Laver's performance in 1969, for which his number is hereby assigned, remains perhaps the greatest year in the history of the sport. Of the thirty-two events in which he competed he won seventeen, including all four Grand Slams, and finished the year with an overall record in singles of 106–16. Such was Laver's dominance of the sport that he was the first player ever to exceed one million dollars in career earnings, and such was his stature in the game that the Centre Court Stadium at

Melbourne Park, home of the Australian Open since 1988, is named Rod Laver Arena and boasts a sculpture depicting him in action on the park grounds. Rod Laver was indisputably the most accomplished men's player of the twentieth century, and in the eyes of the sport's most esteemed chronicler, he was the best player as well. "I remain unconvinced," wrote Bud Collins in his autobiography, "that there was ever a better player than Rod Laver."

"Here comes Willis!"

Those may be the most famous, and beloved, three words in the history of New York sports. With those words, broadcast legend Marv Albert announced that the captain of the Knicks, Willis Reed, was taking the floor to play in game seven of the NBA Finals.

The date was May 8, 1970, and it may well have been the greatest night in the decorated history of Madison Square Garden. The courage of Reed to play through a painful hip injury is what is most often remembered, obscuring what was actually the most remarkable performance of that night, which came from Reed's teammate Walt Frazier, who delivered the greatest game seven in the history of the sport. Frazier played forty-four minutes and finished with 36 points and 19 assists; no other player has ever achieved both of those in any playoff game, much less in the decisive game of the championship series. Further, Frazier delivered his masterpiece against three of the greatest players of all time: Jerry West, Wilt Chamberlain, and Elgin Baylor. The event was the culmination of the greatest season in the history of New York basketball, the city's favorite game. As a New Yorker myself, born and raised, I am fully comfortable asserting that the 1970 World Champion Knicks are the most beloved team the city has ever seen.

The title was the finishing touch on a sensational season that began with wins in twenty-three of the first twenty-four games—the fastest NBA start ever, until Golden State notched

WILLIS REED was the unquestioned leader of the most beloved team New York City has ever seen.

24–0 some forty-six years later. Those old enough to remember can still hear the home fans chanting, "Dee-fense!" for the best defensive team in the league; the Knicks allowed 105.9 points per game that season while no other team allowed fewer than 111. Reed was the unquestioned leader of the group, and was named the league MVP for that season, the only Knicks player ever to win the award. In fact, Reed was the MVP of the regular season, the NBA Finals, and the All-Star Game; only Michael

Jordan and Shaquille O'Neal have achieved that trifecta in the same season. Frazier was fourth in the MVP voting, helping lead New York to sixty wins, a mark the franchise has only ever accomplished one other time.

The Knicks' march to a championship was also remarkable for all the Hall of Famers they faced along the way. In the first round they needed seven games to defeat the Baltimore Bullets, who were led by Earl Monroe and Wes Unseld. Next came the Milwaukee Bucks, featuring a rookie named Lew Alcindor. Finally, the Lakers, with Chamberlain, West, and Baylor. New York was coached by Red Holzman and featured such notable stars as Bill Bradley, Dave DeBusschere, Dick Barnett, and an injured bench player with floppy hair and long arms named Phil Jackson. In my childhood home, those names were spoken with reverence for everything they brought to the city. Mostly, what is remembered is the most famous game in the history of the world's most famous arena, and the legend who made that mark simply by walking onto the floor.

In the entire history of sport, there have been few nights as epic, consequential, and unforgettable as that of March 8, 1971, when two men, both of them giants literally and figuratively, stepped into a boxing ring in Madison Square Garden and changed everything. It was the first time in history that two undefeated champion fighters met for the heavyweight championship of the world. One of them, Muhammad Ali, was and would remain among the most famous people in the world. The other, Joe Frazier, had his hand raised in victory that night, then spent nearly two weeks in the hospital recovering.

It was "The Fight of the Century," with over 20,000 fans in attendance; as historian Bert Sugar would write, "Everybody who was anybody was there." An estimated 300 million more would watch around the globe, including a record 27.5 million in the United Kingdom, approximately half of the British population.

The societal ramifications of that fight, and Frazier's win, have been explored in great depth for half a century, in far greater detail than space allows here. Rather, we will celebrate Frazier himself, not just for his indelible connection to his greatest rival, but for his individual greatness as a champion and a man.

Joe Frazier was the twelfth child born to Rubin and Dolly Frazier, sharecroppers from South Carolina. At fifteen, living in New York and unable to find a job, Frazier began stealing cars and selling them to a Brooklyn junkyard for fifty dollars apiece. Later he found work in a slaughterhouse, where he trained by punching sides of beef in a refrigerated room, providing inspiration for Sylvester Stallone's legendary film

> The only way we know of **ALI**'s greatness is because of **FRAZIER**'s equivalent greatness.
> ~ David Halberstam

Rocky, in which Frazier would make a cameo appearance. In 1964, Frazier became a national celebrity, winning gold in the Tokyo Olympics, despite fighting with a broken thumb in the finals. In all, Frazier would finish his career 32–4–1 with 27 knockouts as a professional, and he would hold a version of the World Heavyweight Championship from 1968 to 1973, reigning as undisputed champion from 1970 to 1973.

It is, of course, his three fights against Ali for which Frazier will forever be remembered, and though he lost two of them, an argument can be made that Frazier's standing was forever elevated nonetheless. No one ever made that argument more eloquently than David Halberstam, the Pulitzer Prize–winning author, when he wrote: "Technically the loser of two of the three fights, [Frazier] seems not to understand that they ennobled him as much as they did Ali. That the only way we know of Ali's greatness is because of Frazier's equivalent greatness, that in the end there was no real difference between the two of them as fighters, and when sports fans and historians think back, they will think of the fights as classics, with no identifiable winner or loser."

It is widely held that the tradition of champagne celebrations
in sports dates back to the 1930s, when champagne merchant
Count Frederic Chandon started offering bottles of bubbly to
the winners of the French Formula One Grand Prix. If true, it
means the popping of corks has been an intrinsic element of
sporting greatness for something like ten decades. In all that
time, my personal favorite celebration is one that still takes
place annually, though the attendance in it has dwindled due
to the inevitable toll taken by the passage of time. Each football
season, when the last remaining unbeaten team falls in defeat,
I love to watch the living members of the 1972 Miami Dolphins
partake in a bubbly commemoration of another year as the
owners of the only perfect season in NFL history.

You likely know that those Dolphins remain the only undefeated Super Bowl champions of all time, finishing 14–0 in the

regular season, then 3–0 in the playoffs. Further, you should know that while there have been five other teams that won championships in undefeated seasons, the only other to do so without any ties was the 1948 Browns, who played in the AAFC. Thus, the '72 Dolphins achieved the only genuinely *perfect* season in NFL history. The teams that came closest to achieving the same distinction include the Patriots in 2007, and the Bears in both 1934 and 1942, all of which entered the championship game with perfect records, only to fall short of winning the title.

> # The '72 DOLPHINS achieved the only genuinely perfect season in NFL history.

What should also be noted is that the Dolphins were not just perfect in 1972, they were also dominant and resilient. The dominance came equally on both sides of the ball; they remain the only Super Bowl champions ever to lead the league in total offense, total defense, scoring offense, and scoring defense. The resiliency, meanwhile, can be summed up in two words: Earl Morrall. Then thirty-eight years old, Morrall began the season as the backup quarterback to Bob Griese, but was pressed into duty when Griese suffered severe leg injuries in a game against San Diego. Morrall led the team to their final nine wins and was named runner-up for league MVP. In all,

Griese started and won six of the team's seventeen games, Morrall the other eleven.

The Dolphins' offense featured five Hall of Famers, including Griese, Larry Csonka, Paul Warfield, Larry Little, and Jim Langer—and let's not forget linebacker Nick Buoniconti on the defensive side. Their coach, Don Shula, would go on to become the winningest coach in the history of the sport. But the achievements of the many, in this case, greatly outshone those of the few, and always will. For as long as any of them are still able, may they pop those corks each and every year with well-deserved pride.

There is no way in the space allotted here—or practically any amount of space for that matter—to do justice to the impact that Billie Jean King has spent a lifetime making, both within and beyond the world of sports. She is a person about whom volumes have been written, and many more will surely come. Consider that in 1975, *Seventeen* magazine polled its readers and found that she was the most admired woman in the world. Golda Meir, the prime minister of Israel, finished second. Fifteen years later, *Life* magazine would name King among the "100 Most Important Americans of the 20th Century." She was the only female athlete on that list. The impact that King had on generations of girls across the world can probably never truly be measured. "She was a crusader fighting a battle for all of us," said Martina Navratilova. "She was carrying the flag; it was all right to be a jock."

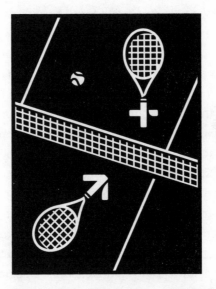

BILLIE JEAN KING

MAY WELL HAVE DONE AS MUCH TO CHANGE
THE WAY WOMEN WERE PERCEIVED IN AMERICAN
CULTURE AS ANY PERSON EVER.

For Billie Jean King, it was more than all right. Through the force of her personality, her extraordinary talent, and her undeniable will, King may well have done as much to change the way women were perceived in American culture as any person ever. When she won her first Wimbledon singles title in 1966, first prize was a certificate for clothing. Seven years later, she founded the Women's Tennis Association and successfully campaigned for equal prize money as the men at the US Open. Through her career she would win over 100 titles in both singles and doubles. In 2009, she was awarded the Presidential Medal of Freedom, the highest civilian honor in the United States.

The number 73 that King is assigned here comes, of course, from her most famous victory, over self-described male chauvinist Bobby Riggs, in the Battle of the Sexes in 1973. The match was played in Houston, in front of 30,000 spectators at the Astrodome, and an estimated 90 million more watching on television, with the legendary Howard Cosell announcing the action. Riggs, a former champion, had boasted that a woman could not withstand the pressure of such a spectacle. King was carried to the court like Cleopatra, and won in three straight sets. It was among the most important nights in the history of American sports, and King herself was well aware of all that was at stake. "I thought it would set us back fifty years if I didn't win," she said. "It would ruin the women's tour and affect all women's self-esteem."

That is quite a burden to carry. It is the reason her autobiography was aptly titled *Pressure Is a Privilege*. There are very few people in sports who can honestly say they changed the world. Billie Jean King is without debate one of those people, and no compilation of this sort could ever be complete without her.

A strong argument could be made that Muhammad Ali is the most significant figure in the history of American sports and, quite possibly, the most important athlete in the history of the world. It's not clear how something like that would be measured, but neither is it apparent to me how any athlete could ever have made a greater impact. As was the case with Billie Jean King, it would be impossible to appropriately tell Ali's story in a format such as this. Instead, we have chosen to focus on 1974, when Ali took part in, and won, two of the most legendary fights in the history of boxing.

Ali first won the heavyweight championship from Sonny Liston in 1964, then had the title stripped away in 1967 after refusing to join the army. He was vilified in many quarters, denounced as anti-American. On January 28, 1974, Ali fought Joe Frazier for the second time, the only one of their bouts that was not for the title. Sandwiched between the Fight of the Century (1971) and the Thrilla in Manilla (1975), the second bout may be the least remembered of the three, but it was by no means the least important. With his victory by unanimous decision, Ali not only avenged the first loss of his career, he also earned a shot to recapture the title.

That shot came on October 30, 1974, in Zaire, against George Foreman, the undefeated and undisputed heavyweight champion of the world. The fight was dubbed "The Rumble in the Jungle" and has been described as the greatest sporting event of the twentieth century. Ali was a significant underdog in the fight, but by employing his "rope-a-dope" tactic for the

A strong argument could be made that **MUHAMMAD ALI** is the most significant figure in the history of American sports.

first time, he earned a stunning victory by knockout in the eighth round. The fight was believed to have a worldwide viewing audience of one billion people, which would mean that roughly one in every four people on planet earth at the time watched it. It grossed approximately $100 million, which would equate to roughly $600 million today. Twenty-two years later, the documentary film *When We Were Kings* told behind-the-scenes stories of the event and won the Academy Award for Best Documentary Feature.

That night in 1974, Ali became only the second man ever to reclaim the heavyweight championship. He would ultimately win it once more, in 1978, and remains the only three-time lineal heavyweight champion in history. The accolades he accumulated over the course of his life include: *Sports Illustrated*'s Sportsman of the Century; the BBC's Sports Personality of the Century; *GQ Magazine*'s Athlete of the Century; the Arthur Ashe Courage Award; and the Presidential Medal of Freedom, the highest civilian honor in the United States. As stated earlier, there isn't any way to do justice to the magnitude of his greatness, or the impact he made upon the world, in this space. Instead, we afford him the final word, as befits a man every bit as renowned for his wit as for his talent:

"I'm king of the world!"

"I'm pretty!"

"I'm a bad man!"

"I shook up the world!"

"I shook up the world!"

"I shook up the world!"

In life, we seldom know at the time that something special is beginning, which is to say that it is only with the benefit of hindsight that we see just how important a given moment may have been. In sports, the NFL Draft of 1969 was that moment. The woebegone Pittsburgh Steelers, perennial cellar dwellers, having not been to the playoffs in over two decades, hired a new coach named Chuck Noll and then selected Joe Greene with the fourth overall pick. Greene would go on to earn one of the best-known nicknames in sports history, and become the foundation upon which was built perhaps the greatest dynasty the sport has ever seen.

Mean Joe Greene was so good so quickly that he was named Defensive Rookie of the Year despite his team being 1–13 and finishing last in scoring defense. It was not long thereafter that the rest of the roster began to catch up, though Greene remained without doubt the most dominant piece of the mighty

Steel Curtain. He made the Pro Bowl in each of his first eight seasons, one of only three defensive linemen ever to do so. He became the first ever two-time winner of the Defensive Player of the Year award, in 1972 and 1974. In Super Bowl IX, the first of the Steelers' four championships in six years, Greene led a defense that held the Vikings to 119 total yards, and only 17 rushing. He was lined up against Hall of Fame center Mick Tingelhoff in that game but still managed to record an interception and a fumble recovery in what is considered among the greatest individual Super Bowl performances ever. Greene would make legendary the number 75 he wore throughout his

MEAN JOE GREENE earned one of the best-known nicknames in sports history and became the foundation of perhaps the greatest dynasty football has ever seen.

thirteen-year career, all in Pittsburgh. He was inducted into the Hall of Fame in his first year of eligibility and was named one of two defensive tackles on the all-time team by the Hall of Fame committee in 2000.

Greene earned his "mean" reputation on the field, occasionally hitting quarterbacks below the knee and in the head, spitting in opponents' faces and kicking them in the groin. Still, he was named the NFL Man of the Year in 1979 for his charitable work away from the field. He also played against type in what may be the most iconic television commercial of all time. If you are old enough to remember, you will never forget the little boy handing Greene a Coca-Cola, nor Greene downing it in one swig, or best of all when he tossed his jersey to the kid, who promptly exclaimed, "Wow! Thanks, Mean Joe!" Those four words brought a Coke and a smile to an entire generation. They also sum up the way every Steelers fan will feel forever about the man who transformed a struggling franchise into one of the greatest winners the sport will ever know.

The game of pro football has been a part of American culture for more than a century, providing the nation with as much enjoyment and as many fascinating characters as any form of entertainment. It would be impossible to definitively select any one person as having been the most important or influential in the long history of the game, but if I had to, I would choose John Madden.

Madden's run as a television analyst may well have been the most significant, and successful, in sports history. For three decades, Madden spent Sunday afternoons or Monday nights making us laugh, making us think, and helping us understand the game in ways we never had before. Madden worked for four networks and instantly elevated each by his presence. He called eleven Super Bowls and won an unprecedented sixteen Emmy Awards. His name is now also synonymous, of course, with one of the most popular video games in the nation. EA Sports' Madden NFL series has generated more than four billion dollars

JOHN MADDEN

MAY WELL HAVE BEEN THE MOST IMPORTANT FIGURE
IN THE LONG HISTORY OF FOOTBALL.

in revenue as of this writing, selling more than 130 million copies—and there is no reason to believe those numbers will slow down any time in the foreseeable future. Madden's name will likely be remembered long after most people who actually watched him on television are gone.

However, for those of us who fell in love with football in the seventies, Madden was never just a voice on TV or a video game; he was forever the coach of the Oakland Raiders, among the most talented and entertaining collections of renegades ever assembled. Madden was an exceptional coach, winning 76 percent of his games over ten seasons, the highest winning percentage in the history of the sport, and thus the number assigned to him here. The Raiders had a winning record in all ten of his seasons and, in fact, had the best record in the sport over the course of his tenure. Madden's best season was in '76, the season in which the Raiders went 13–1 and won the first championship in franchise history; they remain one of five teams ever to win it with one or fewer losses. At forty, Madden was the youngest coach to win the Super Bowl and remained that until Jon Gruden won it twenty-six years later with Tampa Bay. Madden was inducted into the Pro Football Hall of Fame in 2006 for his coaching.

Jerry Jones, the bombastic owner of the Dallas Cowboys, once said "I am not aware of anyone who has made a more meaningful impact on the National Football League than John Madden, and I know of no one who loved the game more." All true. Madden became an icon long after he finished coaching, and his total contribution to the game is far larger than his work on the sideline. But it is as a coach that he earns his place on this list, as he would have wished.

"People always ask, 'Are you a coach or a broadcaster or a video game guy?'" Madden said. "I'm a coach, always been a coach."

Of all the legendary figures celebrated in these pages, there may be none more associated with a particular number than Red Grange. His uniform number, 77, was retired by the University of Illinois after the completion of his final game in 1925, and then again by the Chicago Bears in 1949. Halfway between, in 1937, the immortal chronicler Grantland Rice dubbed Grange's 77 "the most famous number in sport history." Worthy of note is that there was nothing special about the selection of the number; Grange would later say it was chosen for him in college because "the guy in front of me got 76; the guy in back of me got 78."

The statistics Grange amassed in the game's earliest days still boggle the mind. It began in his very first college game when, facing Nebraska, the "Galloping Ghost" scored touchdowns on runs of 50, 35, and 12 yards. The following season, against a Michigan team that was unbeaten in its last twenty games,

Grange scored 4 touchdowns in the first twelve minutes. The touchdowns all came on rushing plays, covering a total of 262 yards. In all, Grange would account for 34 touchdowns in his twenty-four games as a collegian. In 1969, to commemorate college football's centennial, the Football Writers Association of America chose an all-time All-America team. Red Grange was the only unanimous choice. In 2011, the Big Ten Network named him the Number One Icon in the history of the conference.

Grange had no less success as a professional. He was one of four halfbacks named to the 1920s All-Decade team. He led the NFL in touchdowns in 1932, the first season in which statistics were officially kept. He was the star of Chicago's championship teams in 1932 and 1933, catching the title-winning touchdown

RED GRANGE was football's first superstar.

in the first of those on a throw from Bronko Nagurski. Grange was a member of the charter class of the Pro Football Hall of Fame, and the College Football Hall of Fame as well.

Grange was football's first superstar: At the height of his fame there were Red Grange dolls, sweaters, candy bars, shoes—even meat loaf. But Grange did much more than sell merchandise; his brilliance on the field moved the most famous pundits of the era to wax rhapsodic in ways seldom seen in sports history. "This man . . . is three or four men rolled into one for football purposes," wrote Damon Runyon. "He is Jack Dempsey, Babe Ruth, Al Jolson, Paavo Nurmi, and Man o' War. Put together, they spell Grange."

Over the course of my career, I have observed that respect exists between practically all professional athletes, stemming from a tacit understanding of everything it took for each of them to reach the pinnacle of their chosen sports, even if only briefly. I have also seen a special level of regard in which some of them are universally held, the recognition that there are levels, even among the most special among us. In my thirty years in the industry, there is no player I have come across who has engendered the same degree of universal admiration and awe as Anthony Muñoz. And to know him, as I have been fortunate to, is to fully understand why. Not only was Muñoz the greatest offensive lineman to ever live, he is also a person who oozes character, decency, and charisma from every pore.

With the benefit of hindsight, it is hard to imagine that when the Bengals selected Muñoz number three overall in 1980 it was considered a risk. He had suffered multiple knee injuries during his time at USC; Muñoz played only one full game his senior year. As it turned out, he was remarkably durable, missing only three games due to injury during his thirteen-year NFL career, and the impact he made during those years was extraordinary. Founded in 1968, the Bengals had never won a playoff game before he arrived. In the span of Muñoz's career they would win five, reaching the Super Bowl twice, losing both to Joe Montana's 49ers by a combined total of 9 points. In the ten seasons spanning 1981–90, the Niners were the only team to score more points than the Bengals did. Two different Cincinnati quarterbacks won MVP Awards playing behind Muñoz, and both Ken Anderson and Boomer Esiason would

ANTHONY MUÑOZ was the greatest offensive lineman to ever live.

tell you that number 78 was the *real* MVP. In fact, Esiason took it a step further when talking about his decorated teammate: "If I were as good at my position as Anthony is at his, then I'd be ten times better than Joe Montana."

Muñoz was named first-team All-Pro nine times; only Jerry Rice, with ten, has more selections since the merger. No other player in Bengals history has more than three. In the end, Muñoz would be elected to the Hall of Fame in his first year of eligibility, and he remains the only Hall of Famer who spent his entire career with the Bengals. At the turn of the century, he was one of two tackles named to the NFL's all-time team, along with Roosevelt Brown. Ten years later, NFL Network named the Top 100 players of all time, and Muñoz finished twelfth, the highest of any offensive lineman.

Muñoz was named Walter Payton NFL Man of the Year in 1991 for all the good work he had done off the field. To date, his Anthony Muñoz Foundation has awarded more than $2.6 million in scholarships targeted to students overcoming adversity, benefitting more than 50,000 kids. "Have you ever sat down and just thought about how you would want to be remembered as a person?" Muñoz asked. "Not just an athlete or a student, but how you'd want other people to remember you?" In the case of Anthony Muñoz, I can assert from personal experience that people will remember a player as great as any to ever set foot on a field, and a man who was even greater than that.

In the annals of American team sports, there have been few, if any, rivalries more consequential, or delightful, than the one between Larry Bird and Magic Johnson. Their genius, coupled with their animus, elevated the game of basketball to levels of popularity it had never before achieved. The two would meet thirty-seven times as NBA players, with nineteen of those games coming in the finals. But it was a matchup before they even started their NBA careers that truly began it all.

The NCAA Tournament was founded in 1939, but it was not until forty years later that it was transformed into March Madness. Magic and Larry did that. Approximately forty million people watched Johnson's Michigan State Spartans defeat Bird's Indiana State Sycamores in the 1979 title game, good for a television rating of 24.1; it remains the most watched basketball game ever played, college or pro. "It was *Phantom of the Opera* and *Gone with the Wind* and the Olympics all in one,"

IN THE ANNALS OF AMERICAN TEAM SPORTS,
THERE HAVE BEEN FEW, IF ANY, RIVALRIES MORE
CONSEQUENTIAL, OR DELIGHTFUL,
THAN THE ONE BETWEEN
LARRY BIRD
AND **MAGIC JOHNSON**.

said former NBC commentator Al McGuire, whose network televised the game.

Johnson and Bird took their rivalry to the next level, literally and figuratively, immediately after that game. Bird was named the NBA Rookie of the Year in 1980, while Johnson led the Lakers to the championship in that season, scoring 42 points in the title-clinching game six against Philadelphia. Thus began the era of Magic and Larry, polar opposites playing for historical rivals on either coast, and the game has never, ever been better. That "golden era" of the NBA saw the Lakers and Celtics combine to win eight championships in a nine-year stretch, facing each other in the finals three times, Magic winning two of the three and every series lasting at least six games.

In those days, the rivalry between the two was more grudging than it was respectful. "The first thing I would do every morning during the season," Bird says, "was look at the box scores to see what Magic did. I didn't care about anything else." In later years, that dislike dissipated, replaced instead by a beautiful friendship built on mutual respect. As Johnson puts it, "There would be no Magic Johnson without Larry Bird."

On my personal list of the greatest players in the history of basketball, both Johnson and Bird are in the top ten. Each of them individually merits his own place in this collection, to be certain. But in the impact they made together, beyond the statistics they registered or even the championships they won, the two are inextricably linked. In that way, they are simply Magic and Larry, and together they put the Madness in March in '79, before going on to transform the NBA from late night to prime time. I combine their legacies here because the sports fan in me believes they should stand side by side until the end of time.

80

In the months that Hembo and I spent preparin
there were countless occasions where my jaw liter
at the information he provided. The accomplishm
athlete we chose were worthy of both wonder a
none of them—not one—stopped me in my tracks
email with the research notes on the great Jerry
hours trying to figure out how best to present the
able greatness that was his career, and finally co
the best method would be to let you see it exactly
following is an email that arrived in my inbox on I
at 5:06 p.m. The story it tells speaks for itself:

> A strong argument could be made that Jerry
> best football player of all time.
>
> If a rookie recorded 1,000 Rec yds, he would
> it 22 more times to eclipse Rice's all-time reco
> Rec yds).

1,549 career catches (next-most: Larry Fitzgerald—1,432)

22,895 career Rec yds (next-most: Larry Fitzgerald—17,492)

197 career Rec TD (next-most: Randy Moss—156)

208 career touchdowns (next-most: Emmitt Smith—175)

23,540 career yards from scrimmage (next-most: Emmitt Smith—21,579)

23,546 career all-purpose yards (next-most: Brian Mitchell—23,330 . . . but Rice returned 0 punts and 1 kick. Mitchell combined to return 1,070.)

151 postseason catches (next-most: Julian Edelman—118)

2,245 postseason Rec yds (next-most: Julian Edelman—1,442)

A strong argument could be made that **JERRY RICE** is the best football player of all time.

---

22 postseason Rec TD (next-most: Rob Gronkowski—15)

22 postseason TD (next-most: Emmitt Smith & Thurman Thomas—21 each)

2,289 postseason yards from scrimmage (next-most: Thurman Thomas—2,114)

Rice had 1,000 Rec yds in 11 consecutive seasons from 1986–96. No other player in NFL history has done that 11 times TOTAL (let alone consecutively).

Including the playoffs, Rice caught a pass in 302 consecutive games in a span from 1985 to 2004. That is 37 games longer than the next-closest streak (Larry Fitzgerald).

Rice played in 17 postseason wins (equivalent of 1 full NFL season). In those, caught 94 passes for 1,523 yards and 19 TD.

Longevity was extraordinary—if you did not count a single catch he made in his twenties would still have 1,000 catches, 13,546 yards, 102 TD. For context, Randy Moss had 982 catches TOTAL, Torry Holt had 13,382 Rec yds TOTAL, and Tim Brown caught 100 TD TOTAL.

Rice is the only player in NFL history to catch 3 TD in a Super Bowl, and he did it twice. The 49ers accounted for 2 of the 3-highest SB scoring totals in those 2 games.

Rice scored 48 points in his Super Bowl career. The next-most among non-kickers is 30 (Gronk & Emmitt Smith).

2-time Offensive Player of the Year. All other WRs have combined to do it twice (2019 Michael Thomas, 2021 Cooper Kupp)

Rice received 58 MVP votes in the 10 seasons spanning 1986–95. During that time, all other WRs combined for 3.

There were 2 WRs drafted ahead of Jerry Rice in 1985—Al Toon (10th to Jets) & Eddie Brown (13th to Bengals). Those 2 caught 72 TD in the NFL. Rice caught 197.

There really isn't much I can add, aside from saying that the easiest question in sports to answer is: Who is the greatest wide receiver of all time? Jerry Rice is, and likely will always be. He deserves to own the number 80 until the end of time.

A great deal has been made in many places, including here, about the courage and inspiration demonstrated by Willis Reed when he limped onto a basketball floor in 1970 and helped the Knicks win an NBA championship. Well, what if I told you that three decades later, on the grandest stage in American sports, Terrell Owens would bring that same courage and inspiration to an entirely different level? Because, that's exactly what he did. Forty-nine days after sustaining a fractured right fibula and tearing a ligament in his ankle, Owens was the best player on the field in Super Bowl XXXIX. In the buildup to the game, the president of the American Orthopedic Foot and Ankle Society said Owens should not play because he risked doing more serious, even permanent, damage to his leg. But Owens did play, catching 9 passes for 122 yards. And if the Eagles had beaten the Patriots that night, he would have been an easy choice for Super Bowl MVP. Ironically, a player so often accused of being selfish thus authored one of the most selfless performances the game of football has ever seen.

Owens was selected by San Francisco in the third round of the 1996 draft and played his first five seasons with Jerry Rice, the most prolific receiver of all time. Whatever he learned from Rice he obviously put to good use; at the time of Owens's retirement, Rice was the only player ever to amass more receiving yards. Further, Rice, Owens, and Randy Moss are the only receivers in history to score at least 150 touchdowns. Owens was named first-team All-Pro five times in his career; since the merger, Rice is the only receiver to be honored more times.

TERRELL OWENS never failed to put on the show he promised.

During his prime, T.O. was as good as any receiver has ever been. In his lone full season with the Eagles, he set the franchise record with 14 touchdown receptions. While playing for the Cowboys, he averaged 76.3 yards per game receiving, which remains the highest in that franchise's history. Across the full seasons Owens played from 2000 through 2007, he averaged 87 catches for 1,285 yards and 13 touchdowns.

Of course, it is impossible not to notice that, despite all the production, he continued bouncing from team to team, even during the prime of his career. (He played for five teams in total, wearing number 81 for all of them.) Was he indeed a selfish player? A bad teammate? A locker-room cancer? While

I cannot independently answer any of those questions, I *can* tell you that practically every teammate of Owens's I have ever interviewed adores him and vehemently defends his character and professionalism. Candidly, it has never sat well with me that Owens was not elected to the Hall of Fame until his third year of eligibility. I believe the voters held their own biases against a player whose career clearly warranted election in his first opportunity. That Owens then chose to boycott the induction ceremony, instead holding his own celebration at the University of Tennessee–Chattanooga, strikes me as a sad finish to a career worthy of greater fanfare.

The man who famously said "Getcha popcorn ready!" never failed to put on the show he promised. He is one of the genuinely great players in the history of his sport, and well deserving of his place in this collection.

Jack Nicklaus is the greatest ever to play the greatest game ever invented, but when he began it was not his own game that he envisioned. Nicklaus says that, as a young player, when he closed his eyes and visualized the swing he wanted, what he saw was the one that belonged to Sam Snead. The man known as "Slammin' Sammy" had a swing so unique and beautiful it inspired the imaginations not only of other golfers, but of those who chronicle the sport as well. Snead's swing "used to resemble a Faulkner sentence," wrote Bill Fields. "It was long, laced with the perfect pause and blessed with a powerful ending."

Snead was born the same year, 1912, as Byron Nelson and Ben Hogan, and together those legends composed the original "Big Three" of American sports. While Hogan and Nelson are perhaps better remembered today, it could be argued that it was Snead who had the greatest career. He won the 1936 West

Virginia Closed Pro by 16 strokes, which remains tied for the record for any victory at any single event. Twenty-eight years and six months later, he won for the final time—in fact, Snead's longevity is the most extraordinary part of his legacy. He won the 1965 Greater Greensboro Open at fifty-two years old, still the oldest to ever win a PGA Tour event. He finished third at the 1974 PGA Championship at sixty-two, still the oldest to ever finish top ten at any major. And he made the cut at the 1979 PGA Championship at age sixty-seven, the oldest ever to play the weekend at any major. In fact, all seven of Snead's major championships came after he turned thirty; only Nicklaus and Hogan won more after turning thirty.

> # SAM SNEAD was one of the greatest, and most beloved, players in the history of golf.

Snead's number in this compilation comes in honor of his 82 career tour wins, a record he held outright until it was matched by Tiger Woods in 2019; as of this writing, the two remain even atop the all-time leaderboard. For many years, the Tour actually listed Snead's victory total at 84. Then after a 1987 examination, the number was reduced to 81, until it finally settled on 82 after recognizing the Open Championship as an official victory. Interestingly, the Tour also documents Snead winning an additional 62 tournaments that are not part of his official total. In the end, all that quibbling only led us to alter the *number* assigned to Snead, certainly not the worthiness of the man behind it. Sam Snead was one of the greatest, and most beloved, players in the history of golf, and his contributions richly deserve to be remembered forever.

In recent years, the NFL Draft has become among the most anticipated, dissected, and digested events on the annual sports calendar. Having had the privilege of hosting ESPN's coverage of the draft for both television and radio, I have come to understand the two reasons the event is so beloved: In one gathering, the fortunes of every single team in America's most popular sport are dramatically reshaped, while at the exact same time we get to see the wildest dreams of several hundred young men and their families come true right before our eyes. It is reality television that is actually real, and, if you are a football fan, actually *matters*.

Each year the draft tends to be defined by the quarterbacks it produces, thus for the last four decades every quarterback class has been compared to the greatest group the draft has ever seen: the class of '83.

1983

HAS SINCE COME TO BE KNOWN AS "THE
YEAR OF THE QUARTERBACK," HAVING
PRODUCED THE GREATEST CROP OF SIGNAL
CALLERS IN THE HISTORY OF THE GAME.

On April 26, 1983, a record six quarterbacks were selected in round one; it remains the only time that has happened. 1983 has since come to be known as "The Year of the Quarterback," having produced the greatest crop of signal callers in the history of the game.

#1   John Elway—Colts
#7   Todd Blackledge—Chiefs
#14 Jim Kelly—Bills
#15 Tony Eason—Patriots
#24 Ken O'Brien—Jets
#27 Dan Marino—Dolphins

Legendarily, two of the three all-time greats on the list took the road less traveled to history. Elway forced a trade to Denver by threatening to play baseball instead, while Kelly spent two years in the upstart USFL, trying to avoid the cold weather of Buffalo. Ultimately, both wound up right where they belonged, and, along with Marino, completely dominated the sport for nearly two decades. From 1984 to 1998, eleven of fifteen Super Bowls featured a starting quarterback from the 1983 class. (No other collection of first rounders has more than five.) In all, the class combined to make twenty-five Pro Bowls, seven more than any other. Marino and Elway became the first two quarterbacks ever to pass for 50,000 yards in their careers. Kelly, Elway, and Marino were all elected to the Hall of Fame in their first year of eligibility.

Those three legends get a lot of the attention, but they were not the only QBs in the draft class to have successful careers. Only Joe Namath passed for more yards or touchdowns, or won more games, for the Jets than did Ken O'Brien. Tony Eason, meanwhile, led New England to Super Bowl XX, defeating O'Brien and Marino in the playoffs along the way. In total, the 1983 class passed for more yards (204,307) than any other in the history of the sport. The group set a standard that has never been matched, and very likely never will be. While two of the icons have their own place in this collection, it only seems right that they should all be remembered together as well.

For the great LeBron James, we have selected 84 in honor of the year of his birth, largely because I think it is an incredibly important part of his story, particularly in the way he is perceived. (Explanations to come *after* we give "The King" his just due.) Because he is still so much at the epicenter of our sports universe, it hardly seems necessary to run through all James's accomplishments, so the following is a partial list of one of the greatest résumés in the history of sports, updated as of this writing in the summer of 2022.

- One of four players with at least four MVPs and four titles, the others being Kareem Abdul-Jabbar, Michael Jordan, and Bill Russell.
- Reached the NBA Finals in eight consecutive years; the only others to do so all played for the Celtics in the 1960s.
- First-team All-NBA thirteen times, most in history.

- Top five in MVP voting thirteen straight years, longest-ever streak of its kind.
- 48 career playoff games with 30 points, 10 rebounds, and 5 assists; Kareem ranks second all-time, with 20 such games.
- Eighteen seasons averaging 25 PPG, 5 more than any other player ever.
- Only player ever to win Finals MVP for three different teams.
- Opened the I Promise School in 2018, specifically focused on outreach to at-risk youth in his hometown, and arranged for students who complete the school's program to have free tuition at the University of Akron.

LeBron James was on the cover of *Sports Illustrated* when he was seventeen years old. Two weeks before his eighteenth birthday, ESPN televised one of his high school games solely because he was playing. LeBron came into the NBA straight from high school as the most hyped prospect of all time, and somehow managed to eclipse even the most impossible expectations. And yet, for all of those, he has been the most criticized immortal in the history of American sports. That is, in my view, completely unfair. It is also a sign of the times in which he has lived, hence the significance of his birth year. Consider, LeBron is the first millennial to achieve the status he has in sports. Bear in mind that as of December 2021, he has literally spent half his life as an NBA player. Making his career in the confluence of those two factors has been his greatest burden, and in my judgment, he has carried all that weight with dignity. I can tell you with great confidence that Michael Jordan would not have managed nearly as well had his every misstep been dissected and dwelled upon the way LeBron's have.

I suppose we cannot leave this without engaging, even if briefly, in the laziest and most overused debate in sports. If you have ever listened to me on the radio or television, you are already aware that I am team Michael. That is dictated, more than anything, by my age. Jordan will always be the one for me mostly because I was younger then, and everything was better when we were younger. Oscar was my father's Michael. LeBron is my son's; he and his friends refer to James as "LeGoat." All of those are subjective, and in the right spirit can be good fun to talk about. Objectively, the only reasonable thing one can say

> Despite eclipsing even the most impossible expectations, **LEBRON JAMES** has been the most unfairly criticized immortal in the history of American sports.

about LeBron James is that as a ballplayer he is about as good as any that ever lived, and that off the court he has conducted himself with enormous intelligence and class. All the millions of hours of content he generates have their place, but they only belong around the edges of what he has accomplished as a player and a man.

In the fall of 1985, I moved from New York to the Chicago suburb of Evanston to attend Northwestern University. This was a time, of course, before there was an extended NFL package of any sort on television; the games that were on regular TV were the games that we watched. There were no other options. Which explains why this Jets fan saw every single snap taken by the Chicago Bears that season. They were the best team I ever saw play in any sport, and brash enough to record the "Super Bowl Shuffle" song before the playoffs had even begun. They were true Monsters of the Midway, and they left absolute destruction in their wake.

Consider that the Bears outgained their opponents in eighteen of their nineteen games that year, including the playoffs. The game in which they were outgained came in week four against Washington, and the Bears won 45–10; they remain the only NFL team ever to outgain their opponents eighteen times in any season. They are also the only team since the adoption of the sixteen-game schedule in 1978 to score over 400 points and allow fewer than 200. Their final scoring margin of +339 remains the greatest in pro football history.

The head coach and spiritual leader, Mike Ditka, was named Coach of the Year in 1985 and became a folk hero in the city of Chicago. He was Da Coach of Da Bears—in many ways he still is; his shadow has loomed large over every coach the team has employed since. The offense was led by Walter Payton, who had over 2,000 yards from scrimmage, as well as quarterback Jim McMahon, who did not lose a single game he started that

When the games got bigger, the **CHICAGO BEARS** got better.

season; McMahon's fourteen wins without a loss are the most for any quarterback in the Super Bowl era. The defense was led by Mike Singletary, who was named Defensive Player of the Year, as well as Richard Dent, who led the NFL in sacks (17) and forced fumbles (7) and was the MVP of the Super Bowl. That defense was coordinated by the legendary Buddy Ryan and is remembered today as the famed "46 Defense." (It remains my contention that if the Bears had punted on first down every time they got the ball, they would have finished 8–8—*that* is how dominating that defense was.) By the way, kicker Kevin Butler, a rookie in 1985, led the NFL in scoring with 144 points.

When the games got bigger, the Bears got better. They remain the only team to record two shutouts in a single postseason. In all, they allowed 10 total points in their three playoff games in '85. The defense did not allow a touchdown until the fortieth drive of those playoffs; they were leading 44–3 in the Super Bowl at the time. At the NFL's centennial, the 1985 Bears were named the second-greatest team ever, behind the unbeaten Dolphins of 1972. I suppose that is fair; perfection is perfection after all. I know that lone defeat against Dan Marino's Dolphins on a Monday night still eats at many of the Bears players, who otherwise would have been an obvious choice for number one. The blemish does not, however, change the way I view that group, nor the fondness with which I remember them. Go ahead and line up any football team ever assembled, and I will gladly bet you everything I have that the 1985 Bears would shuffle all over them.

It has always struck me as fascinating that some of the best teams ever to take the field of play are largely remembered for being so many things other than that. In the case of the '86 New York Mets, however, it is eminently understandable; being a dominant team on the field was, by no means, the most interesting thing about that traveling circus headquartered in Queens, New York. The collection of outlandish personalities, the drinking, the drugs, the fights, all have stood the test of time. So, of course, has the impossible manner in which they stayed alive in game six of the World Series, as mythically described by Vin Scully: "A little roller up along first . . . behind the bag. It gets through Buckner! Here comes Knight, and the Mets win it!"

What has to some degree been lost, though, is that the 1986 Mets were among the handful of greatest teams in National League history. That they did not feature a collection of Hall of Famers, like the dynastic Cincinnati Reds of a decade before, should not obscure the fact that, for one season, they dominated in a manner few teams ever have. The Mets went 108–54 that season; the only teams in National League history to win more games had been the 1906 Cubs (116) and the 1909 Pirates (110). The Mets finished 21.5 games clear of the second-place Phillies in the National League East, spending 170 days in first place in the division. They finished the regular season with a +205 run differential; the next-best team in the National League was +85.

> For the **'86 METS**, being a dominant team on the field was, by no means, the most interesting thing about that traveling circus.

While Gary Carter is the only member of the team to be inducted into the Hall of Fame, the Mets had numerous players who compiled brilliant seasons. For starters: all of their starters. The 1986 Mets had four pitchers that won at least fifteen games *and* 70 percent of their decisions—Dwight Gooden, Ron Darling, Bob Ojeda, and Sid Fernandez. The last team to do that was the 1927 Yankees. All four of those Mets pitchers received at least one Cy Young vote; the rest of the NL had four combined. In total, six different Mets players received at least one vote for MVP.

The magic-carpet ride that was the team's postseason remains the stuff of legend. To advance to the World Series, the Mets needed twenty-eight innings in two days to eliminate the Houston Astros in six games. Then, of course, came the series against the Red Sox, and the miracle comeback in game six, perhaps the most famous rally in the history of the sport. But the '86 Mets are cemented as legends well beyond their home city not just because of the magical way in which they won, but also because of the larger-than-life way in which they went about their business. "No matter what the media said about us, we all had fun," said Darryl Strawberry, the star-crossed superstar of the team. "We liked the attention, of course, but we brought our best to the ballpark. That's what the fans loved about us. We had swagger and we won."

When tight end prospect Rob Gronkowski came to visit the New England Patriots ahead of the 2010 NFL Draft, he took a nap on the floor while wearing a suit that cost fifteen hundred dollars. In a show of extraordinary judgment, the Patriots selected him anyway. Thus was born one of the most productive relationships in the history of pro football, between a buttoned-up quarterback and a lovable goofball tight end, both of whom turned out to be the best ever at their respective positions.

"What you see is what you get," Tom Brady said of his favorite weapon. "Whether he is dancing, singing, laughing, or spiking, he is true to himself." I have, in fact, occasionally wondered if Gronk's larger-than-life personality has distracted fans from recognizing his greatness; he is the best tight end ever to play the game, and it isn't even close. He may actually be the greatest red zone target in the history of the game, regardless of position.

Simply put, few people have ever been better at anything than number 87 was at catching touchdowns.

He is the only tight end to catch 10 touchdowns in five different seasons, which he did during his first six seasons in the league. Over that span, he caught a total of 65 touchdowns—only Jerry Rice and Randy Moss had more through six years. In fact, during those first six seasons in the league, Gronk scored more touchdowns (66) than any player in the NFL regardless of position. His 17 touchdowns in 2011 are the most by a tight end in NFL history. Including the playoffs, he caught 20 that season, also the record for his position. In the biggest games, Gronk got

> **GRONK**'s larger-than-life personality has distracted fans from recognizing his greatness; he is the best tight end ever to play the game.

even bigger. Only Jerry Rice caught more touchdowns in the postseason. In fact, Gronkowski and Rice are the only players with multiple receiving touchdowns in multiple Super Bowls. And there is one category in which even the great Rice could not keep pace: Gronk is the only player in NFL history to catch a pass in five different Super Bowls.

Tom Brady had a special chemistry with many receivers

during his brilliant career, most notably Wes Welker and Julian Edelman, not to mention a record-breaking season with Randy Moss. But there is no debate over who was Brady's favorite target. Through the 2021 season, Brady had thrown 105 touchdown passes to Gronkowski, and no more than 41 to anyone else. Those 105 touchdowns stand second all-time of any NFL duo, behind only Peyton Manning and Marvin Harrison. The postseason record, meanwhile, belongs to Brady and Gronk, with 15 touchdown connections (as of this writing).

Bill Belichick once described Gronkowski as a "coach's dream," and it is to Belichick's everlasting credit that he never held back Gronk's boisterous nature. Perhaps the young tight end never really gave the coach a good reason to. After all, as Brady said, "He is obviously the greatest tight end ever to play the game."

On January 30, 1971, UCLA beat UC Santa Barbara in men's basketball by a score of 74–61. On January 17, 1974, the same Bruins beat Iowa 66–44. Those wins were separated by 1,083 days and not one single defeat; John Wooden's teams won 88 games in a row, a record that stands to this day and seems extremely unlikely to ever be broken.

That stretch of basketball, overseen by the coach known as the Wizard of Westwood, compares favorably with any period of domination in the history of American sports. The Bruins outscored their opponents by 2,064 points over those 88 games, meaning their average margin of victory was 23 points. They had more wins by at least 30 points (28) than they did single digits (16). They were the number one team in the AP Poll for forty-six consecutive weeks, nineteen longer than the next longest streak in history.

The streak is perhaps the most remembered of John Wooden's accomplishments at UCLA, but it is far from the only one. There has simply never been a coach as dominant in any sport as Wooden was. Geno Auriemma has come the closest, along with Nick Saban, Phil Jackson, Mike Krzyzewski, and Bill Belichick. Times have changed substantially enough that the accomplishments of all of those coaches may well compare favorably with Wooden's when viewed in a broader context. But, still, the numbers are the numbers—and they are astonishing. Wooden coached four undefeated national championship teams; all other coaches in Men's Division One history have combined for

> # JOHN WOODEN's 88-GAME
> win streak with UCLA
> is a record that seems
> unlikely to ever be broken.

three. Wooden won seven consecutive national titles; no other coach has won as many as three in a row. During that span, from 1967 to 1973, Wooden's teams won seven championships and lost a combined total of five games. Overall, Wooden never had a losing season, after taking over a UCLA program that had been 286–283 all-time before his arrival.

Wooden's coaching career became the stuff of such legend that his playing career has been largely forgotten. He led Purdue to the national championship in 1932, seven years before the first NCAA Tournament. He led the National Basketball League in scoring in 1932–33, thirteen years before the NBA was founded. He was inducted into the Hall of Fame as a player in 1960, thirteen years before he was voted in as a coach, and became the first person ever inducted as both. Better remembered, of course, are Wooden's iconic Pyramid of Success and his easily digestible inspirational quotes known as "Woodenisms." Among those, my favorite is this: "Success is peace of mind, which is a direct result of self-satisfaction in knowing you did your best to become the best you are capable of becoming."

89

Being a league that emphasizes the star power of its players, it is no surprise that the NBA has a logo depicting the silhouette of Jerry West. By the same token, as the NFL is a league that emphasizes teams over individuals, it is equally unsurprising that its logo is a faceless shield. It has long been my contention, however, that if pro football were ever to consider using a familiar image as its logo, it could do no better than selecting the singular visage of Iron Mike Ditka.

The very first assignment for which I was ever paid was the Bears' draft in 1991 at Halas Hall. I will never forget the moment Ditka walked into the media room to talk about the team's first-round selection of Stan Thomas. There was an electricity, an aura, around Ditka that I've seldom encountered in anyone else in all my years covering sports. A generation later, I worked with Ditka at ESPN: We broadcasted two NFL games together, and he appeared on *Mike and Mike* every week for more than a decade. I have deep affection and admiration for the man, no matter how differently he and I occasionally see the world.

All that said, Ditka's legend grew so large as a coach, analyst, and personality, that what is too often forgotten is that he was the first great tight end in NFL history, and one of the best players that ever lived. It began at the University of Pittsburgh, where his jersey number, 89, is retired in his honor. Then on to Chicago, where his rookie season was truly one for the ages. Ditka remains the only tight end ever to be named Rookie of the Year, honoring a season in which he had 1,076 receiving

> # If pro football were to consider using a familiar image as its logo, it could do no better than the visage of **IRON MIKE DITKA.**

yards and 12 touchdowns. Six decades later, those marks both remain the rookie records for the position. The next rookie tight end to catch even 10 touchdowns was Rob Gronkowski in 2010; the next to amass 1,000 receiving yards was Kyle Pitts in 2021. In his third season, the Bears won the NFL Championship, and Ditka led the team in receptions, yards from scrimmage, and touchdowns. Ultimately, he became the first tight end to be inducted into the Pro Football Hall of Fame, and his number

89 was retired in Chicago, just as it had been at his alma mater.

Ditka's coaching career, of course, brought him greater rec-ognition and fame than he enjoyed as a player. In the eight seasons spanning 1984–91, Ditka was the winningest coach in the sport. He remains the only Hall of Fame player to win more than a hundred games (121) as a head coach. He is also the only player in the modern era to win a title with the same team as both a player and head coach, which goes a long way toward explaining the affection he receives from his adopted hometown of Chicago. The "Super Fans" sketches on *Saturday Night Live*, while hilarious, were actually a fairly accurate rep-resentation of the way Bears loyalists felt about Ditka—how they still feel to this day.

Among the many fond memories I will take to my grave of Mike Ditka, my favorite is an expression he used frequently: "Whether you think you can, or you think you can't, you're right." Mike Ditka always thought he could, and in the entire history of professional football there weren't too many people more right about anything than he was about that.

If you are like me—and judging by your decision to buy this book, I suspect you are—while you may very well not remember what you ate for breakfast this morning, you will never forget *exactly* where you were sitting when you watched the most memorable sporting events of your lifetime. I certainly do. I remember watching Bernard King score 60 on Christmas Day from the blue seats at Madison Square Garden. I remember watching Michael Jordan's game six masterpiece in the 1998 NBA Finals in an ESPN newsroom that no longer exists. I remember watching the Northwestern men's basketball team play its first ever NCAA Tournament game in Salt Lake City, with my wife and kids cheering their lungs out beside me. All those were especially memorable to me because of personal connections—I'm sure you don't recall them all the way I do. However, if you are old enough, I will wager everything I own that you remember precisely where you were the night of February 11, 1990, when Buster Douglas knocked out Mike Tyson. It was, and remains, the most shocking event I have ever witnessed in a lifetime spent watching sports.

Tyson was not just the undefeated, undisputed heavyweight champion of the world at the time; he was something far greater than that, a modern-day myth. The way he would enter the ring with zero pageantry, all business and intimidation. The ferocity with which he took apart every fighter he faced. The raw power of his punches—when he knocked out Michael Spinks in the first round in 1988, he didn't just become the champion, he became a legend. Now it was just twenty months after that

> **MIKE TYSON,** the undefeated, undisputed heavyweight champion of the world, was also something far greater than that: a modern-day myth.

fight, and he was in Tokyo facing a virtual unknown in what was perceived to be a tune-up for Tyson's eventual showdown with Evander Holyfield. Tyson was installed as a 42–1 favorite in Las Vegas for the Douglas fight; by comparison, when Cassius Clay "shook up the world" by knocking out the heavily favored Sonny Liston, Clay was only a 7–1 underdog.

I was in the living room of my parents' apartment in Southern

California, a world away from the action, when, in the tenth round of a stunningly even fight, Douglas rocked Tyson with a right uppercut, then followed with a four-punch combination that sent the champion to the mat. Then the seemingly invincible Tyson was crawling along the canvas, groping for his mouthpiece in the corner, sticking it in sideways, stumbling to his feet. He was counted out at 1:23 of the tenth round. It was the first defeat of his professional career, after thirty-seven victories, thirty-three by knockout. The great Jim Lampley delivered an unforgettable call: "Mike Tyson has been knocked out! Let's go ahead and call it—the biggest upset in the history of heavyweight championship fights! Say it now, gentlemen, James Buster Douglas—undisputed heavyweight champion of the world!"

One of the best reasons to love sports is that there is no script. On any given night, you never know what might happen. You never know which night might become like that one in 1990, when the impossible happened, and you spend the rest of your life marveling at the thrill it was to behold.

begin this section with an admission: I could not *stand* Dennis Rodman when he played for the Bulls. I was around those teams day in and day out and found Rodman to be the ultimate self-promoter who delighted in grabbing every ounce of the spotlight provided by the brilliance of Michael Jordan and milking it for purely self-serving reasons. I could not have cared less about his dalliances with Madonna or Carmen Electra, his wedding dress, his multicolored hair, or, candidly, anything else about his life away from the court. That said, he genuinely was an extraordinary player and a vital piece of those three championship teams. It is his own fault that history does not remember his play as kindly as it should; his combination of self-absorbed nonsense and occasional dirty play tend to overshadow the things that made him special.

Rodman had already won two titles as number 10 with the Bad Boy Pistons by the time he was traded to Chicago in October

1995. The Bulls had previously retired the jersey number 10 in honor of Bob Love, and thus did Rodman select 91, because the digits added up to ten. The trade was met with great skepticism in Chicago because of Rodman's history of cheap shots against Bulls players. The concern didn't last long. What was quickly obvious to everyone was that Rodman was far more than just the rebounds he grabbed, which were seemingly endless in number. His passing, defensive intensity, and overall basketball IQ were off the charts. I am willing to say, albeit through clenched teeth, that the Bulls would not have won any of those three titles without him.

> I am willing to say, albeit through clenched teeth, that the Bulls would not have won any of their last three titles without **DENNIS RODMAN**.

While his numbers did not tell the whole story, his numbers were, nonetheless, ridiculous. Rodman led the NBA in rebounding all three seasons he played in Chicago, something he did for seven straight seasons from 1992–98, the longest streak of its kind in NBA history. His three years remain the three highest rebounding seasons in Bulls history. In the 1996 postseason, Rodman was the Bulls' outright leading rebounder in each of their last fifteen games en route to the title. He grabbed eleven *offensive* rebounds twice in the finals that year; all other players in NBA Finals history have combined to do it once. (Elvin Hayes, in 1979.) Rodman's contribution was quintessentially unique: he pulled in 3,036 rebounds in his three regular seasons in Chicago, 304 more than any player in the NBA, while 239 players scored more points than he did during those years. In 2021, Rodman was recognized as one of the seventy-five greatest players in NBA history, the only player on the list who averaged fewer than 10 points per game.

Rodman's post-career behavior has, of course, been even more distasteful, including his unconscionable relationship with Kim Jong-Un. Were I taking those sorts of things into account, there is no way Rodman would merit inclusion here. But fair is fair. Rodman deserves his place in the Hall of Fame based upon his enormous contribution to five NBA championship teams, and he deserves his place here as well.

One of the most important career decisions any athlete has ever made looks very different today, when observed in the rearview mirror of history. It was April 6, 1993, just at the advent of NFL free agency, when the best defensive player in the sport chose to take his talents to Green Bay. Today that hardly seems like an earth-shattering call to make, but what cannot be over-looked is the context in which the decision took place. Brett Favre had played only one season for the Packers, and while he showed promise, there was no way to know he would prove to be among the greatest quarterbacks of all time. Meanwhile, that tiny town in Wisconsin was not a desired destination for practically any player of the era. "It was Siberia," said former Packers tight end Keith Jackson. "But Reggie White saw some-thing different about it."

White, who became an ordained minister at the age of sev-enteen, would say God told him to go to Green Bay. And the rest, as they say, is history. The Packers had been to the play-offs only twice since Vince Lombardi led them to the first two Super Bowl championships, but they made the postseason in each of White's six seasons in Green Bay, winning Super Bowl XXXI over the Patriots in a game in which White sacked New England quarterback Drew Bledsoe three times in the second half. When the game was over, White famously ran around the Superdome carrying the championship trophy, creating one of the most indelible images in the history of pro football.

REGGIE WHITE became the first player ever to have his number retired by two franchises.

That title was the pinnacle of what was among the greatest careers in the history of the NFL. It began in Philadelphia, where White played under the legendary Buddy Ryan. In the strike-shortened season of 1987, White registered 21 sacks in just twelve games, which remains the most in any season with twelve or fewer games played. In all, he recorded 124 sacks in 121 games for Philadelphia, still the franchise record. He added 68.5 more in Green Bay and retired as the all-time leader with 198, a mark since surpassed only by Bruce Smith. For his consistency and brilliance, White became the first player ever to have his number—92—retired by two franchises.

Meanwhile, his total list of accomplishments remains astounding. White remains the only player with at least

10 sacks in nine consecutive seasons. He was named the Defensive Player of the Year in 1987 and then again in 1998; that eleven-year gap is the largest of its kind in NFL history, and White remains the only player to win the award playing for two different teams. He was named first-team All-Decade in the 1980s *and* 1990s by the Pro Football Hall of Fame. In 2000, he and Deacon Jones were named the defensive ends on the NFL's All-Time team. In 2006, White was elected to the hall in his first year of eligibility.

Tragically, the election was posthumous; White died in 2004 of a cardiac arrhythmia at the age of forty-three. The magnitude of his loss, considering the force of his personality and universal respect he engendered, cannot be overstated. However, his legacy on the field remains cast in stone, as was one of his greatest desires. "The thing that I know, and everyone else knows, is that no one can ever take my accomplishments away," White said. "My goal as a football player was to be the best to ever play my position. I believe I've reached my goal."

93

ople to name the most memorable C
o team and they are likely to mentio
t won seventy-two games, or the 19
ast dance for Michael Jordan and c
ing this book to find out what most p
to tell you that the '93 title was Jord
and it capped the greatest three-yea
dern NBA ever saw.

set the stage, because I was there. Tl
title in 1992, after a slugfest of a fil
lan was exhausted when that serie:
y needed a summer of rest to recharg
ummer of the Dream Team. The trut
t of Barcelona, but despite the fact the
on gold without him, neither the NI
llow such an historic event to take pl

their biggest star. Thus, reluctantly, the exhausted Jordan spent his summer in the pressure cooker that was that experience, not because there was any competition on the floor, but because the environment around the team was something akin to Beatlemania. Jordan returned to Chicago for the following season without any of the rest he desperately needed.

By now you know how it ended, with the most dramatic playoff rounds imaginable, ending with the Bulls facing the Knicks and the Suns back-to-back. New York, led by Patrick Ewing, jumped to a 2–0 lead in the Conference Finals, the only time Jordan would ever trail by more than one game in a series during the championship years. He led them back, of course, scoring 54 points in game four to even the matter

> The '93 TITLE was
> MICHAEL JORDAN's
> greatest achievement.

and eventually disposing of the Knicks in six. Next came the league MVP, Charles Barkley, and his Suns. Phoenix had set a franchise record for wins that season. This time, Jordan's team struck first, winning the first two games on the road. Barkley led the Suns back and the series became an absolute classic; in the six games of those finals the teams scored the exact same number of points (640). The Bulls did not post a single double-digit victory in the series. Many remember that John Paxson hit the game-winning three-pointer in the decisive game six in Phoenix, but they should be reminded that those were Chicago's only points of the fourth quarter that Jordan did not score.

In the end, that postseason saw the Bulls defeat three players that finished top five in MVP voting, five that finished top ten, seven all-stars, and four All-NBA players. Jordan averaged 35.1 points per game in the playoffs and 41.0 in the finals, the most in NBA history. By the end, he was spent. When he retired prematurely a few months later, I was saddened but not surprised. It had taken literally everything he had to accomplish the threepeat, something the sport had not seen since the days of Bill Russell. Even Jordan, the greatest there ever was, simply had nothing left to give.

94

The Olympics are the pinnacle of human athletic accomplishment, an ancient tradition that is generally considered to date back to at least 776 BC, and very possibly several centuries before that. However long the history may be, I think it is safe to say that there has never been an Olympic event more anticipated, dissected, and scrutinized than the 1994 Women's Figure Skating competition in Lillehammer, Norway. Ironically, Lillehammer, the northernmost city ever to host an Olympic games, was the setting for the final act of one of the most lowdown and dirty episodes in Olympic history.

You are no doubt aware of Nancy Kerrigan and Tonya Harding, their names forever linked through one of the most infamous acts in the history of international sports. Harding remains among the most controversial athletes ever to represent the United States, while Kerrigan, through no fault of her own, will always be remembered as much for the worst moment of her career as for the utter triumph that was the silver medal she won on the Norwegian ice. The relationship between the two of them has inspired films, television series, documentaries, books, and hundreds of millions of internet clicks. There is no part of the story I can tell that will shed any new light on the sordid affair. Instead, I will share an account that was told to me on a podcast by broadcasting legend

1994 was an unforgettable year in sports, but it belongs to NANCY KERRIGAN.

Verne Lundquist, who anchored CBS's coverage of figure skating during those games. His recollection provides a fascinating insight into the magnitude of an episode that history will never forget:

"It was a cartoon. The afternoon that they both appeared on the Olympic arena ice together for the first time, I still vividly remember, here were the following CBS News teams in the building: Martha Teichner, CBS News; Bill Geist, CBS News; Mark Phillips, CBS News; Susan Spencer, CBS News; and directly beneath our perch, Connie Chung co-anchored the evening news with Dan Rather.

"Overkill? Perhaps. But then they skated, and the next day the overnight ratings came in and 48.5 percent of the television sets in the United States were tuned in; our estimated audience was 126 million."

Lundquist is a man who has seen it all. And even he never saw anything like Tonya and Nancy.

1994 was an unforgettable year in sports, for more reasons than we can recount. In June, America watched O. J. Simpson lead police in Los Angeles. I vividly recall my shock hearing the words "O. J. Simpson is possibly armed and dangerous." I went home after the soccer game and, like everyone else, watched my boyhood idol in a white Ford Bronco, leading the police on a slow chase along a California freeway.

The following month, a Colombian soccer player named Andrés Escobar was murdered, reportedly as retaliation for having scored an own goal that led to his team being eliminated from the World Cup. Just twenty-seven years old, Escobar's nickname on the pitch was "The Gentleman."

In August, Major League Baseball's players went on strike, causing the cancellation of the World Series. It remains the only year since 1904 that the Fall Classic was not contested, including all the years of both World Wars.

Amid all the drama and turmoil of that year in sports, the triumph of Nancy Kerrigan in Norway stands alone for me. With the eyes of the world upon her, and despite all she had been through, Kerrigan skated brilliantly, winning silver, and many believe she should have won gold. In fact, had any of the four judges scored her 1/10th higher, she would have brought the gold medal home. It is patently unfair that she be remembered for the worst moment of her year rather than the best, and equally unfair that her name should always appear alongside Harding's. Nancy Kerrigan doesn't deserve that. What she deserves is for her accomplishment to outlast her unwitting infamy. She deserves a place in this collection all to herself; finally, number 94 belongs only to her.

"And let it be said, that number 8, Cal Ripken Junior, has reached the unreachable star!"

With those words, my colleague Chris Berman perfectly crystalized a moment no baseball fan thought would ever come. On September 6, 1995, as that evening's game between the Orioles and California Angels became official, so did Ripken break one of the records that seemed certain never to fall: Lou Gehrig's streak of consecutive games played.

The record was fifty-six years old. Gehrig was, and remains, known as the Iron Horse of American sports, which made the toppling of his mark one of the greatest accomplishments of all time. Consider: If you were to add together the streaks of the players who are third and fourth on the list, Everett Scott and Steve Garvey, they would still be 118 games below where Ripken left the record at 2,632. For further perspective, 3,713 major league players went on the disabled list during the thirteen years that it took for Ripken to pass Gehrig. Also, as Ripken played both shortstop and third base during the streak; 781 other players played at least once in one or the other of those positions during that span.

"Wherever my former teammate Lou Gehrig is today," the legendary Joe DiMaggio told Ripken, "I'm sure he's tipping his cap to you, Cal. You certainly deserve this lasting tribute." That is right on many levels, not the least of which is that the record was made far more special by the greatness of Ripken's career. Gehrig was, of course, way more than an Iron Horse; he was also the greatest first baseman in the history of the sport—a

> # CAL RIPKEN JR. did as much to connect with fans as any player I ever saw.

combination that made his streak so legendary. Similarly, Ripken was not merely durable, he is on the short list of greatest shortstops ever to play. He was the American League Rookie of the Year in 1982, and the league MVP the following year as he led the Orioles to a World Series championship. He finished with two MVP Awards, as well as eight Silver Slugger Awards and nineteen all-star selections, the most in AL history. He retired as one of seven players ever with 400 home runs and 3,000 hits. He was elected to the Hall of Fame on the first ballot in 2007 with 98.5 percent of the vote. Candidly, any writer who didn't vote for him should never have been allowed to vote again.

"I never really allowed myself to think about the streak," Ripken would say. "It was very simple; I wanted to come to the ballpark, I wanted to play, I wanted to help the team win." That is the enduring legacy of Cal Ripken Jr. I can still picture the swarms of kids and autograph seekers he patiently entertained, doing as much to connect with fans as any player I ever saw, both before and after the strike that canceled the 1994 World Series. He treated people with respect and the game with reverence, both exactly as they should be. Even if the impossible ultimately happens and his streak is someday broken, no telling of the history of baseball could ever be complete without him.

If I were asked to choose my single favorite statistic in sports history, it would take me absolutely no time to respond with: More men have walked on the moon (twelve) than have scored an earned run off Mariano Rivera in the postseason (eleven).

Mind you, that is with Rivera having pitched in 96 post-season games, a record that seems highly unlikely ever to be approached. In those 96 games, Rivera took the loss a total of once, while recording 42 saves and an ERA of 0.70. In twenty-two of the thirty-two series in which he pitched, he did not allow a single earned run. He was a five-time champion and remains the only pitcher ever to record saves in three World Series–clinching games, which he did in three consecutive years.

"Rivera is definitively the best at his position by a wider margin than any player at any position in the history of baseball," wrote esteemed baseball columnist Tom Verducci. "There is

MARIANO RIVERA's
CUTTER RANKS ALONG KAREEM'S SKYHOOK
AS ONE OF THE MOST UNSTOPPABLE WEAPONS
IN THE HISTORY OF SPORTS.

Rivera, a gulf, and then every other closer." Of that, there is no room for disagreement, seeing as Rivera's dominance was by no means limited to the playoffs. He is baseball's all-time regular-season leader in ERA, saves, and games finished. His 1,115 appearances are the all-time record among right-handed pitchers. Further, he is the only man ever to pitch in more than 1,000 games for a single team. And he did it all, essentially, with one pitch. Rivera's cutter ranks alongside Kareem Abdul-Jabbar's skyhook as one of the most unstoppable, unbeatable weapons in the history of sports. "You know what's coming," an opposing hitter once said. "But you know what's coming in horror movies, too."

In 1995, Rivera and teammate Derek Jeter were both sent down to Triple A by the Yankees, who seriously considered trading Rivera. There are no records kept of greatest trades never to happen, but it's hard to imagine one better. In 1996, Rivera helped pitch the Yankees to the first of four World Series crowns in five years; it is from that season, along with his 96 playoff games, that his number here was selected. After all, his uniform number was 42; he was the last player ever to wear the digits retired across the sport in honor of Jackie Robinson. The other number to consider with Rivera would be 0, which is the number of baseball writers who chose not to elect him to the Hall of Fame. Rivera was the first and only player ever to be voted in unanimously. Obviously, many other players have deserved to be so honored, but if anyone had to be the first, there could hardly be a more worthy candidate. "Probably not since Koufax," said Hall of Famer Joe Torre, Rivera's longtime manager in New York, "have we seen anyone leave the game with so much respect."

I have worked at ESPN since the fall of 1996, and there is no doubt that in that time Tiger Woods has been the most dominant and culturally significant athlete in the world. His ascendancy began just a few months after I got to Bristol, in April 1997, when Tiger obliterated the field at Augusta to officially begin the transformation from phenom to immortal. At the age of twenty-one, Tiger won the Masters that spring by 12 shots, which remains the largest margin of victory at the event and the largest margin of victory for any golfer's first major championship. Tiger still remains the youngest ever to earn the fabled Green Jacket, setting twenty Masters records that week and tying six others. He also became the first non-white athlete to win the most tradition-bound event in sports; it truly was "a win for the ages," as Jim Nantz called it on CBS.

Tiger would, of course, go on to dominate the sport in a manner unlike anyone ever. His apex was higher than anyone else's, including Jack Nicklaus. Lest anyone question that, consider that Nicklaus won thirty events before turning thirty, which was the record until Tiger won *forty-six* times before his thirtieth birthday. Tiger also clinched the career Grand Slam at age twenty-four, two years younger than Nicklaus had. Candidly, if his body had not broken down, it is a safe bet to assume that Woods would currently hold every significant record in the sport.

Instead, as of this writing, Tiger sits tied atop the all-time wins list with eighty-two, and three off Nicklaus's record of eighteen majors. Those are the most prominent statistics of

> # TIGER WOODS has been the most dominant and culturally significant athlete in the world.

his career, but they are in no way the most astounding. Here are a few that are a great deal more fun:

- There are five instances of a player winning at the same PGA Tour tournament seven times. Tiger has four of those five.
- There are three instances of a player winning eight times at the same course. Tiger has all three.
- Over the last seventy years, there are three instances of a player winning five consecutive starts. All of them were Tiger Woods.
- Since 1900, there are only two instances in which a golfer

won a major by ten or more strokes—Tiger at the 1997 Masters and Tiger at the 2000 US Open.

- Since 1999, Tiger has won at least five PGA Tour events in ten different seasons. No other golfer has done it more than once over that span.
- Tiger spent 683 weeks as the number-one-ranked player in the world, the most ever. Greg Norman is next, with 331.

Tiger Woods has been so famous for so long for so many reasons that, at times, it is hard to keep track of them all. The narrative arc of his career, and his life, have frequently felt Shakespearian. But one thing has never wavered, and that is the utter thrill of watching him play the game of golf. For me, he is the most compelling athlete of his generation by a wide margin. It has been a privilege to chronicle every shot he's ever hit, and in honor of the year in which it all began, number 97 belongs to him.

98

Working, as I do, at ESPN, I am forever surroun
on televisions. Some of it is current, much of
Either way, it is safe to say that within my vision
practically all times is a monitor showing images
among all the videos I ever come across, there is
looks more different today from the way it origin
than images of Mark McGwire and Sammy Sosa p
ultimately, surpassing the home run record in 1

Every ounce of the joy and electricity I vivid
from that time has been wrung from the screer
lemon, leaving behind something limp and di
empty. Which is exactly as it should be. That ma
turned out to be an illusion, unworthy of bein
though steadfastly impossible to forget.

I have heard it said that the best way to gauge w
a player belongs in the Hall of Fame is by asking t

Can you tell the story of the history of the sport without him or her in it? It is that logic I have applied in making this selection. McGwire and Sosa dishonored the game, to be sure, but there is no way to tell the story of baseball without them. That is what the voters for the Hall of Fame have gotten wrong, in my opinion. Trying to write a history that omits what those two sluggers did in '98 is to turn fact into fiction. The simple truth is: It happened. And no one who watched what they did will ever forget them.

> # MARK MCGWIRE and SAMMY SOSA dishonored the game of baseball in 1998, but there is no way to tell the story of baseball without them.

The summer of 1998 was unlike anything I ever witnessed in my lifetime. McGwire and Sosa entered the month of September with 55 homers apiece. McGwire then hit 7 more in as many games, breaking Roger Maris's record on September 8. That record had stood for thirty-seven years, still the longest the single season mark has ever lasted.

McGwire and Sosa entered the final weekend of the season tied at 65 home runs. Sosa briefly took the lead on September 25, hitting his last home run of the season; it was the only time he was first in MLB history to any number, the 66 he finished with. McGwire would hit five more over the final three games to finish with 70. Overall, McGwire held at least a share of the lead for 136 straight days. Sosa never led outright at the end of any calendar day; in fact he only led outright for a total of 103 minutes, taking the lead from McGwire twice, only to see McGwire reclaim a share of the lead within an hour each time.

Today, people are fond of saying that McGwire and Sosa "saved" baseball. I find this notion a tad insulting. Certainly they brought an element of excitement to a sport that needed *something* after the strike canceled the 1994 World Series. But to suggest they saved the sport is, to me, to pretend that no one else ever would have. Baseball is too wonderful a game, and too deeply ingrained in our society, to have remained dormant. Someone was going to do something that saved it sooner or later. McGwire and Sosa were just in the right place at the right time. That time was 1998, and while it will never feel the same, it remains a memory worthy of keeping, and a number they will share forever.

Wayne Gretzky is the greatest athlete in the history of North American team sports.

Yes, he is. For the simple reason that the gap between Gretzky and whomever might be considered next on the NHL list (Lemieux? Howe? Orr?) is undeniably greater than between the greatest players in any other sport. For instance, I believe Michael Jordan to be the top in basketball, but I understand that an argument could be made for Kareem Abdul-Jabbar, and further I am aware that credible people have reached the conclusion that LeBron James is Jordan's equal. Similar points can be made in other sports. None can be made in hockey. The Great One is the greatest one, and no one sees it any other way.

Where does one begin to describe this man's career? I suppose at the very beginning, with a newspaper headline that read: *Hull, Richard, Howe and Gretzky.* Wayne was nine years old when that comparison was made. Then, there were, of course, the four Stanley Cups in five years, from 1984 to 1988. Gretzky's

WAYNE GRETZKY

IS THE GREATEST ATHLETE IN THE HISTORY OF
NORTH AMERICAN TEAM SPORTS.

Oilers teams in that era dominated like few others in sports history. Consider: There have only ever been five 400-goal seasons in the NHL, and they were *all* achieved by Edmonton, in consecutive years from 1982 to 1986. Gretzky's trade to Los Angeles might trail only Babe Ruth's to New York in terms of consequence to any sport; *Edmonton Sun* columnist Graham Hicks explained the fans' devastation succinctly: "He was our best reason for living here."

In his career, Gretzky would receive the Hart Memorial Trophy (MVP) nine times. Barry Bonds is the closest in any other sport to matching that with seven. Gretzky is the all-time leader in goals (894) and assists (1,963), and thus, naturally, points (2,857). He tallied 936 more points than any other player all-time, meaning he would be the all-time points leader even if he had never scored a single goal. Gretzky owns each of the top seven seasons in history in assists, and eleven of the top thirteen. He is also the only player ever to exceed 90 goals in any season, and the only player to tally 200 points in a season, which he did four times.

When Gretzky retired, the Hockey Hall of Fame waived the mandatory waiting period and inducted him in November 1999, just seven months after he played his final game. The following year, the NHL retired his iconic number, 99, league-wide, the ultimate testament to the unimaginable, and unprecedented, greatness of the Great One. As is true for many of those chosen for this list, there isn't any way to fully do justice to Gretzky's genius, or his impact, in such little space. Perhaps best to leave it to a prominent Canadian hockey fan to offer the final words. "If you look at a grandmaster in chess," said author and journalist Malcolm Gladwell, "he can look at a chessboard and he doesn't see twenty individual pieces. He sees a sequence. That's the same thing going on about Gretzky."

100

egendary individual performance in the
orts took place in Hershey, Pennsylvania, w
 spectators in attendance. Those folks w
who would ever see it, as the game was not
on, and no video footage has ever been disc
as March 2, 1962. The teams were the Phila
d New York Knicks. And the performer was
hamberlain, who scored 100 points, a rec
and will never, be broken.
d and colleague Jalen Rose always says, "Th
 books, the one for Wilt and the one for eve
's the best explanation I have heard for th
e of the legendary big man. If I had the s
y list 100 things he accomplished on the ba
no one else ever will. For instance, in that se
ad the 100-point game, "The Big Dipper" av
s and 25.7 rebounds per game. He also av

playing 48.5 minutes, as he was on the court for 4,458 of his team's 4,466 minutes that season, including the playoffs. He missed those eight minutes after an ejection, meaning he was not substituted out of a single game all year. He did not win league MVP that season, by the way, proving what his future teammate Jerry West would famously bemoan: Nobody ever roots for Goliath.

Chamberlain owns each of the top four scoring seasons in NBA history, and each of the top three in rebounding. He averaged 35 points and 20 rebounds in five consecutive seasons; no other player has ever done that once. There are five instances in

> # The obscurity of the **100-POINT GAME** has only served to add to its legend.

history in which a player scored 30 points in twenty consecutive games; Chamberlain did it four of those five times (James Harden the other). There are three instances in which a player scored 40 points in ten consecutive games; Chamberlain has all three such streaks. There are four instances in which a player scored 50 points in five consecutive games; Chamberlain has all four. My favorite of all the stats is this: Hakeem Olajuwon is the all-time leader in blocked shots—because blocks did not become an official statistic until 1973–74, the season after Chamberlain retired. The record is 3,830, despite the fact Chamberlain is unofficially credited with 9,300 blocks.

The obscurity of the 100-point game has only served to add to its legend. No members of the New York press were present, none having bothered to make the trip. Further, not only was the game not broadcast on television, but the original radio call on WCAU was recorded over by an engineer, as was standard practice in those days. It was not until decades later that any copies were discovered. As for Chamberlain himself, we offer the final word to the legendary Johnny "Red" Kerr, who played both with and against Wilt during his career. "He was the NBA," Kerr said. "He was the guy on the top. He was the most dominating center—the best center to ever play in the NBA."

FINAL WORD

So, there they are, the hundred (or so) heaviest hitters in history. They are presented with no expectation of agreement; issues as personal as these are seldom met with nodding heads. So let the arguments spew forth. Have them with me if you like, but, even better, have them amongst the people you care about, all the ones who care about this stuff, too. Those people who, like us, understand that there is nothing in the world better than to invest everything you have into something that means absolutely nothing. I actually wrote that thought—the bit about investment—in my first book, fifteen years ago, and if anything I believe it even more strongly today. These games that people play are the best possible escape for those of us who understand their unique significance, and they come now at a time when most of us need that more than ever.

So, by all means, have at it. Pick apart my list from the top to the bottom. I will gladly defend every word I've written. But, in true sports talk fashion, I will also always listen to your side.

ACKNOWLEDGMENTS

Thank you to everyone at Team Greeny, including: David Larabell and the entire crew at CAA, Nick Khan, Mark and Jason Bradburn, Richard Koenigsberg, Diane Johnston, and Erika Echavarria. Thank you to everyone I am privileged to work with at ESPN—the passion and professionalism you bring to our shows every day inspires me more than you will ever know. Most of all, thank you to everyone who has ever chosen to watch me on TV, listen to me on the radio, or read the things I write; I don't have words to adequately express the gratitude I feel for all the fun we've had together.